THE 5-INGREDIENT ITALIAN COOKBOOK

THE 5-Ingredient ITALIAN COOKBOOK

101 REGIONAL CLASSICS MADE SIMPLE

FRANCESCA MONTILLO

PHOTOGRAPHY BY DARREN MUIR

ROCKRIDGE PRESS

Interior and Cover Designer: Merideth Harte
Photo Art Director: Amy Hartmann
Editor: Kim Suarez
Production Editor: Andrew Yackira
Photography: Photography © 2018 Darren Muir. Food styling by Yolanda Muir.
Author photo: Wicked Shots Photography
Illustrations: Merideth Harte

ISBN: Print 978-1-64152-307-3 | eBook 978-1-64152-308-0

To my mom, Celeste, who never tires of me asking "how-to" cooking questions. And to my sister, Roseanne, who always insisted that I write a cookbook. Thank you for the support!

CONTENTS

What is Italian Cooking? **viii**

1
Italian Essentials for American Kitchens
1

2
Antipasti e Contorni
Appetizers and Sides
13

3
Zuppe e Insalate
Soups and Salads
31

4
Risotto, Pasta, e Salse
Risotto, Pasta, and Sauces
47

5
Pizza e Pane
Pizza and Bread
67

6
Carne
Meat
85

7
Pollo
Chicken
99

8
Pesce e Frutti di Mare
Fish and Seafood
115

9
Dolce
Desserts
131

Glossary **151**
Italian Courses **153**
The Dirty Dozen & the Clean Fifteen™ **154**
Measurement Conversions **155**
Recipe Index **156**
Index **158**

WHAT IS ITALIAN COOKING?

Hello!

I was born in Italy and, as my luck would have it, into a family that valued home cooking and family meals. From an early age I was welcomed into the kitchen. This is not so unusual in Italy; in fact, it's very much the norm. While my mom was the primary cook, my dad had a small business as a greengrocer, so both parents really instilled an appreciation for fresh ingredients, home-cooked meals, and family time. We were surrounded by loved ones at the table, and discussions frequently flowed around what we would be having at our next meal! It's not surprising that my most beloved memories of growing up in Italy are an appreciation of food and family.

Home Is Where the Heart Is

Home cooking is very much a part of daily life in Italy. Far more than just another daily chore, cooking, and ultimately sharing meals with family and friends, is always cause for celebration for Italians. Family meals occur daily—not just on distinct holidays or special occasions. Families use mealtime as a way to catch up and discuss the day's activities over a delicious meal. Italians love home cooking, and while Italy doesn't lack for great restaurants, far more meals are eaten at home than out. Ask any Italian where their favorite place to eat is, and their response will likely be "my mother's!"

Italian cooking is very seasonal, and many ingredients, especially vegetables, are rarely eaten out of season. Zucchini, green beans, eggplants, and tomatoes are the kings of the summer season, while broccoli and broccoli rabe, cauliflower, potatoes, and mushrooms are more widely used in fall and winter months. Italian cooking is known for its simplicity and ease of preparation, and many dishes contain only a handful of major ingredients. Italian cooking relies on quality and freshness rather than processed and convenient or complex and elaborate.

A Regional Cuisine

In addition to being seasonal, Italian cuisine is very much regional. A dish that's commonplace in southern Italy may be relatively unheard of in northern Italy. We would be hard pressed to find one dish that is prepared the same way throughout the country. The 20 regions of Italy make use of what they have most readily available, which makes sense given the emphasis on freshness and using local ingredients as much as possible.

With miles and miles of olive trees, southern Italy's fat of choice is olive oil, and people rarely use butter for cooking. Northern Italians, however, do use butter and cream in cooking heavier sauces and dishes. Surrounded by the Ionian, Tyrrhenian, and Mediterranean seas, Sicily boasts a hefty repertoire of seafood dishes, while regions such as Tuscany thrive on meats, especially wild boar and beef. *Chianina*, for example, is a local breed of cattle used to make the famous Florentine steaks. Pasta is another example of regional contrasts. Stuffed pasta such as tortellini and ravioli and specialties like egg tagliatelle are commonplace in the northern city of Bologna; however, southern Italians tend to prepare homemade pasta with just durum wheat flour and water.

Less Is Always More

When it comes to authentic Italian cooking, the quality of ingredients far outweighs quantity. Traditional Italian recipes don't call for a laundry list of miscellaneous ingredients; instead you'll find carefully selected items that complement each dish in a meaningful way. Each ingredient adds something of value to the dish, be it flavor, texture, or sustenance. As such, it's easy to prepare dishes with five main ingredients or fewer, as everything used offers maximum flavor. Seasonality is key, as is freshness.

Italian American dishes, on the other hand, frequently call for adding heavy sauces and using lots of garlic—far more than is actually used in Italy. Everything appears to be topped off with grated cheese. Salads are dressed with "dressings," as opposed to extra-virgin olive oil and some red wine vinegar. Indeed, in Italy some of these ingredients are used, but they are not used to the extent that we in the United States think they are. We've grown accustomed to using these flavor enhancements, and have come to call any dish "Italian" that uses them. While these dishes may be Italian inspired, and perhaps no less delicious than authentic Italian food, they may not be what Italian cooks prepare at home. In the United States, sometimes we have a tendency to add ingredients "just because." I'm happy to show you that less is always more when it comes to home-style cooking in Italy.

REGIONAL MAP OF **ITALIAN CUISINE**

NORTHWEST

Trentino-Alto Adige

NORTHEAST

Valle d'Aosta

Lombardy

Friuli-Venezia Giulia

Veneto

Piedmont

Emilia-Romagna

Liguria

Marche

CENTRAL

Umbria

Abruzzo

Tuscany

Molise

Lazio

Puglia

Campania

SOUTH

Sardinia

Basilicata

ISLANDS

Calabria

Sicily

Northwest

Somewhat influenced by France, its bordering neighbor, the cuisine of northwest Italy, consisting of the Valle d'Aosta (Acosta Valley), Liguria, Lombardy, and Piedmont, is earthy, unique, and rich. Mushrooms such as truffles are heavily enjoyed in Piedmont. Fontina cheese is the preferred cheese of the Valle d'Aosta. Risottos are popular in Lombardy, where they are often prepared in a buttery, creamy sauce. Pesto alla Genovese (page 50) is probably one of Liguria's most famous dishes. Thanks in part to its proximity to the water, Liguria also enjoys a wide variety of seafood dishes—tuna, sardines, and bass are just a few of the regional favorites.

Northeast

The cuisine of the northeast regions, consisting of Emilia-Romagna, Friuli–Venezia Giulia, Trentino–Alto Adige, and Veneto, tends to be a bit heavier and denser. Meaty Bolognese sauce is devoured in Emilia-Romagna; hearty polenta in wild boar sauce is enjoyed in Trentino. Prosciutto San Daniele, from the town of San Daniele in Friuli–Venezia Giulia, is used in stuffed pastas, over pizza, and in sandwiches. Risi e Bisi (page 53) and Pasta e Fagioli (page 61) are beloved dishes in Veneto.

Central

Central Italy consists of Tuscany, Lazio, Marche, and Umbria. Tuscans enjoy simply prepared dishes without added seasonings or flavorings; in fact, even their bread is unsalted. They enjoy a *bistecca* (steak) simply grilled, and lots of beans and legumes. Like much of Italy, Lazio, which is home to Italy's capital, Rome, also favors simple cuisine over elaborate dishes. There, Pecorino Romano is the cheese of choice, either in chunks or grated, and pasta dishes are easy and simple, such as Amatriciana-Style Bucatini (page 59). The people of the Marche region often prefer vegetables and legumes to meat dishes, and a favorite of theirs is Chickpea Soup (page 41). Umbrians pride themselves on their pork products, and for good reason—they are highly praised all over Italy, and their Pasta alla Norcina (page 62) is frequently served both at home and at restaurants.

South

Peperoncino, olives, capers, red onions, and hefty doses of dry pastas are what you will find in the southern regions of Abruzzo, Puglia, Basilicata, Calabria, Campania, and Molise. Fresh vegetables are seasonal and abundant. Pork is the meat of choice, and fish is a widely served second course. Olive oil is the fat mostly used, as opposed to butter, to sauté meat, fish, and pastas, and is often used in dressings for salads and vegetables.

Islands

Fresh, healthy, nutritious, and nourishing are all words to describe the cuisine of Sardinia and Sicily. Fish and quality produce reign supreme in the Italian islands, and olive oil, seafood, fresh fruits and vegetables, and locally made cheeses are always on the Sicilian and Sardinian table. Ricotta is used in both savory and sweet dishes and desserts, including cannoli, and cassata cake. Lemon Granita (page 148) is a refreshing treat in Sicily.

Italian Recipes for American Tables

Replicating Italy's home-style cooking shouldn't be difficult for Americans; if you follow the guidelines provided in this book, it will come rather easily. Carefully selecting ingredients that are fresh and in season is key. Cheese for grating should be as fresh as possible. Avoid pre-grated cheeses, as they often contain fillers. High-quality olive oil that is appealing to your palate is also a must, so before selecting one for continued long-term use, you may want to try out a few bottles.

While this book is divided into dishes, as opposed to courses, please feel free to "mix and match" as you wish. An appetizer might make a wonderful light lunch, and focaccia bread can be used for a delicious panino. You can adapt as you see fit.

ITALIAN ESSENTIALS FOR AMERICAN KITCHENS

If you have ever visited Italy, or even eaten in an Italian American household, I am sure you noticed that when it comes to Italian cooking, the quality of ingredients makes the meal. It's amazing what a few basic, high-quality ingredients can turn into. In this book, you will be introduced to key ingredients used in Italy that are readily available in the United States, as well as techniques and strategies that make cooking more efficient and streamlined. With these recipes, Italian cooking has never been easier!

The Pantry

As you go through this book, you will find that the recipes call for common ingredients that are likely already in your pantry. These ingredients are versatile for multi-recipe use, and having them in your pantry will prepare you for making many wonderful meals for your family.

Fresh and Perishable:

Onions and garlic: No Italian pantry would be complete without these two staples. Store them separately in mesh containers or in a box that has breathing holes. Keep them in a cool, dry place and be on the lookout for any sprouts.

Potatoes: Used in many Italian dishes, potatoes should be stored in a cool place, away from onions. Onions exude gases that accelerate the spoilage and sprouting of potatoes.

Dry nuts: Many baking recipes require dry nuts. While nuts are perfectly safe to store at room temperature for about a month or so, you'll want to refrigerate them if you will not be using them within a month, or they will likely turn rancid from the oil they contain.

SHOPPING FOR VEGETABLES & FRUITS

Shop in season: Seasonal produce is tastier, healthier, and more sustainable than those that are out of season. Visit the farmers' market for seasonal harvests.

Keep it fresh: Most fruits and vegetables expire quickly, so avoid stocking up too much. Plan your meals a few days in advance and just purchase items as needed.

Plan resourcefully: Italians are as frugal as anyone, and in addition to shopping in season, they also shop the sales! Look for deals and specials and plan your meals from there.

Be discriminating: Use your senses when selecting produce. Fruits should be free of any obvious bruises or blemishes. Green vegetables should be bright green; avoid any that are turning yellow, wilting, or shriveling—sure signs that the produce is getting older.

Spices:

Peperoncino: Used especially in southern Italian cuisine, peperoncino, or red pepper flakes, are a must in Italian cooking, especially in many dishes from Calabria or Sicily. Adding both flavor and heat, pepper flakes should definitely be used according to preference.

Nutmeg: Used frequently in potato dishes or fillings for tortellini or ravioli and in other Italian dishes where a nutty flavor is desired.

Dried oregano: While technically an herb and not a spice, dried oregano is a must for a good Italian pantry. It adds lots of flavor, and just a wee bit goes a long way. Quick tip: Rub it between your fingers before adding it to your dish to release the oils.

Pickled or Canned Items:

Canned tomatoes: High-quality canned tomatoes are an invaluable ingredient. A component in most red sauces, canned tomatoes of various sizes should be added to your pantry (see Choosing Quality Ingredients, page 5).

Oil: Few Italian dishes omit some sort of oil. Used in all kinds of cooking and preparation, from sautéing and frying to dressing salads, olive oil is a staple you'll want to have in stock at all times. Invest in buying several bottles at once (see Choosing Quality Ingredients, page 5).

Canned beans and chickpeas: Used in countless soups all over Italy, canned legumes are convenient, inexpensive, satiating, and quick to cook (see Choosing Quality Ingredients, page 5).

Vinegars: Italians don't have much use for what we know as salad dressing. Dressing a salad in Italy usually involves a simple combination of high-quality oil and some sort of vinegar, be it red wine, white wine, or balsamic. A squirt of lemon juice is sometimes added. In addition to salads, vinegars are frequently used in cooking meats (see Choosing Quality Ingredients, page 5).

Capers: Used frequently in southern Italian cuisine, especially dishes from Sicily, this robust little flower bud is inexpensive and adds lots of flavor and some saltiness to your dishes.

Dry Goods:

Dry pasta of various types and dry tortellini: For an Italian, a day without pasta is almost a crime! This economical staple is a must in your pantry (see Choosing Quality Ingredients, page 5). Dry pasta comes in thousands of shapes and sizes, from long pasta, such as spaghetti and fettuccini, to short pasta such as ziti, penne, and elbows. Dry tortellini are also a welcomed quick addition to many soups or first courses.

Rice: Used in preparing dishes such as risotto, Risi e Bisi (page 53), and soups, rice is a staple that many Italians rely upon.

Polenta: Eaten plain or dressed in sauces, rich or simply prepared, polenta (cornmeal) is a wonderful, adaptable alternative to mashed potatoes and is sometimes even served as a first course.

All-purpose flour: Used to make pizzas, focaccias, and baked goods; thicken sauces; and flour meat or fish before frying, all-purpose flour is an ingredient that is required in many daily dishes.

The Refrigerator & Freezer

A well-stocked refrigerator means one less trip to the grocery store. Here are some items to keep on hand for easy preparation during busy weeknights.

Refrigerator

Cheese for grating: Be it a chunk of Parmesan (from cow's milk) or the saltier, sharper Pecorino Romano (from sheep's milk), or ideally both, grated cheese is used in countless Italian dishes. If buying an entire piece is not an option, ask the clerk at the deli counter to grate some for you. Avoid highly processed, pre-grated cheese.

Italian flat-leaf parsley: Fresh herbs such as parsley, basil, rosemary, and oregano add a lot of wonderful flavor to your dishes, but if you must select just one to keep on hand, make it Italian flat-leaf parsley. It will add freshness and a hint of color to any dish. It's ideal for cooking or decorating a plate before serving.

Bread crumbs: While it's perfectly fine to keep bread crumbs in the cupboard instead of the refrigerator, I, along with many Italians, refrigerate them in order to extend their life. Choose high-quality bakery bread crumbs whenever possible— they are far superior in flavor to other options. Also, select unflavored crumbs (no added parsley or seasonings) so you can adjust the level of the flavoring accordingly.

CHOOSING QUALITY INGREDIENTS

Italian cooking frequently relies on products such as olive oil, balsamic vinegar, and canned tomatoes. Since quality matters in successful Italian cooking, here are some tips for purchasing commonly used products:

Olive oil: I generally use extra-virgin olive oil (EVOO) when eating it "raw"—to dress a salad, drizzle over grilled meats and vegetables, or add to soups after cooking for added flavor. For cooking, use regular olive oil (sometimes labeled simply "olive oil" or "pure olive oil") when cooking. Much of the strong flavor is lost when cooking with EVOO, and since it's more expensive, it might not be financially worth it to cook with costly EVOO. Truth be told, I believe they can be used interchangeably very easily, as I often do. It depends on budget and whether someone would rather not have more than one bottle in the kitchen. Recommended brands include Newman's Own Organic EVOO, Bertolli, Colavita, Carapelli, and Whole Foods.

Canned tomatoes: San Marzano are a great variety of canned tomatoes but are not available in all stores. Recommended brands of canned/crushed tomatoes include Pomi, Cento, Pastene, and Muir Glen.

Balsamic vinegar: Traditional balsamic vinegar is only made in Emilia-Romagna from reduced Trebbiano or Lambrusco "grape must" (by-products of pressed grapes). It is aged for 12 to 18 years or more, free of added colors, and is a regulated ingredient certified by a Protected Designation of Origin. It's also thick and syrupy, and for many, its high price tag makes it an expensive luxury. Commercial balsamic vinegar is not regulated, does not have an aging requirement, and is made all over the world with various grapes. This kind is still delicious and has many uses, and of the many brands available, I recommend Colavita, Newman's Own Organic, and Whole Foods.

Dry pasta: Keeping dry pasta on hand allows you to make crowd-pleasing meals on the fly. I recommend De Cecco, Garofalo, and the easy-to-find Barilla.

Canned legumes: Beans are used often in soups and salads, and the canned variety is handy. My top choices are Goya, Progresso, and Cento.

Italian tuna: Italian tuna is packed in olive oil, making it much more tender and flavorful than regular tuna. I love Genova and Pastene brands. Look online or in stores near you that carry these.

Butter: While southern Italians prefer olive oil, northerners use butter to flavor risottos or to sauté meats or vegetables. Keep the unsalted version on hand for baking and the salted version for savory dishes.

Fresh vegetables: Broccoli, broccoli rabe, cabbages, green beans, celery, carrots, and Swiss chard are only a few of the vegetables found in Italian and Italian American refrigerators. These perish quickly, so be sure to schedule your meals accordingly to avoid waste.

Freezer

Peas: When it comes to frozen vegetables, Italians definitely have a preference for peas. Economical, practical, and savored by the young and not so young, peas are added to soups and stews, risottos, and the famous Risi e Bisi (page 53). They last for several months in the freezer, so store a few bags.

Chicken: Be they cutlets, tenders, or bone-in chicken, keep some portions in the freezer for a quick chicken Marsala or chicken with lemon and capers. Boneless cuts are ideal for weeknight meals as they are easy to prep and cook. Bone-in, while equally tasty, requires a longer cooking time.

Frozen basil: It's perfectly acceptable to freeze some fresh herbs when in season and abundant. Although parsley can be found year-round, fresh basil is seasonal and can get expensive when out of season. Buy some during the summer, rinse it, dry it on paper towels, and freeze for winter soups and stews.

Pizza dough: In chapter 5 you will find a super easy recipe for Basic Pizza Dough (page 68). This dough freezes well, so be like the rest of the Italians and freeze some for future use. It's very common for Italians to reserve some "in case of emergency," or when the mood strikes and there's no time to let it rise.

Stock: Used frequently in soups and risottos and as a quick flavor booster. Make a fresh batch of Quick Vegetable Broth (page 39) and store in plastic containers for freezing.

Tomato sauce: Homemade tomato sauce freezes very well, and in chapter 4 you will learn to prepare a super easy version (page 48). Freeze some in small containers and have it ready whenever needed. Use it as a simple dressing for pasta, add it to soups, or a pizza—homemade sauce makes everything special.

- Do you have tomato sauce left over? Add it to soups or stews for extra flavor and a hint of color. Leftover sauce should be refrigerated in an airtight container for up to four days or frozen for up to several months.
- Leftover pizza (if there's ever such a thing) is never wasted. Wrap it tightly in aluminum foil and reheat the next day in a toaster oven, oven broiler, or a cast iron pan or skillet on the stovetop.
- Don't let that Parmesan rind go to waste. Filled with flavor, that rind can be added to soups, stews, or sauces. Although it's perfectly edible if it breaks down, discard large pieces before serving. Store Parmesan cheese in an airtight container or tightly wrapped in aluminum foil in the refrigerator.

- Day-old bread is never wasted in Italy, and it's perfect for making homemade bread crumbs. Make sure the bread is completely dried out by leaving it on the counter for a few days, then put it in a food processor and pulse until it resembles crumbs. Bread crumbs can be stored in an airtight container in the cupboard but will stay fresh longer refrigerated.
- Garlic and onions are staples in Italian cooking. They should be stored in a cool, dry place—even a basement—and never in plastic bags or the refrigerator, as they require ventilation. Also, keep onions away from potatoes, as onions speed up sprouting in the potatoes.

The Equipment

A well-equipped kitchen makes the cooking process more efficient and enjoyable. Here's a list of must-have items:

Colander: All cooks (especially pasta-eating Italians) will benefit from several colanders of varying sizes and shapes to drain pasta and rinse vegetables. In addition to sizes, be sure to look at the holes. They should not be too big, which will make straining small pasta shapes impossible, nor too small, which will make straining vegetables difficult.

Sauce, soup, sauté, and stock pans: A small collection of saucepans and soup pots is ideal for making red sauces as well as for boiling pasta and vegetables. A high-quality stainless steel collection of various sizes will last for years to come. Unlike other materials, stainless steel is ideal for storing foods overnight in the refrigerator.

Cutting boards: Wooden or plastic, the kind you select is up to you, but keep several boards on hand—one marked for chicken or meat use only, one for fruits and vegetables, and another for breads or dry goods. Clean boards, especially the meat one, very thoroughly.

Wooden spoons: Italians seem to have a fascination with wooden spoons, and most households have a very large collection of this inexpensive and practical tool used for stirring soups, stews, and sauces. Start growing your own collection!

The Core Techniques

Quality ingredients and great tools will only get you so far. You'll need to master a few basic techniques in order to prepare some delicious meals.

Boiling: Boiling is a basic technique that entails cooking an ingredient in water or stock over high heat on the stovetop. Pasta, grains, potatoes, and other vegetables are some of the most common foods that call for boiling. Reducing the heat while boiling will result in what is called a simmer. To bring things to a boil faster, cover the pot with a lid.

Sautéing: One of my preferred methods of cooking boneless chicken breasts or fish, sautéing involves cooking ingredients in a hot pan with a little fat, such as oil or butter. This method is also ideal for cooking down onions when starting risottos or tomato-based sauces. Many soups incorporate onions, celery, and carrots sautéed in olive oil. You will see many recipes in this book that call for sautéing.

Roasting: If you are pressed for time and can't stay at the stove to stir a pan of food, roast foods in the oven instead. Roasted foods are uncovered (for maximum heat exposure) and are cooked at high temperatures for a crisp or caramelized texture or at lower temperatures for a more tender texture. It's an ideal way to cook vegetables such as potatoes, carrots, or Brussels sprouts, and all sorts of meats.

Baking: Baking also involves using the heat from the oven for cooking, but almost always at lower temperatures. In addition to the focaccia, pizzas, and desserts you'll find in this book, Italians bake lasagnas, stuffed shells, and seafood. The key to successful baking is testing your oven temperature with an oven thermometer to make sure it's calibrated properly.

Frying: Frying calls for cooking food in a fat source, like oil, over high heat. Similar to sautéing, frying uses much more fat (the food being fried is frequently covered in the fat). In Italian cooking, we frequently fry cutlets or vegetables, resulting in a very crispy finished product.

The Recipes

Now that you've got the basics down, it's time to bring the scent of the old country to your kitchen and prepare some delicious dishes.

In my years of teaching Italian cooking, I've noticed that what students appreciate the most are not "special occasion" recipes that take hours to prepare, but everyday recipes—the kind that you can easily replicate at home. It's fun to come to a cooking class and learn something new, but the appeal wanes quickly if you will never prepare what you made at home because it's too complicated, calls for hard-to-find ingredients, or feels otherwise too complex to attempt on your own.

The recipes in this book are approachable, nonintimidating, and easy to prepare. Many take 30 minutes or under, and best of all, every recipe contains five or fewer main ingredients. All the ingredients are multipurpose, so there's no need to worry about having leftover ingredients—you will be able to use them in other recipes. You'll also notice that the recipes offer a nice blend of some popular dishes that you likely have heard of, as well as many lesser-known homestyle dishes, meant to be prepared by home cooks and served to hungry families. This combination of dishes will give you a large and varied Italian culinary repertoire you can be proud of.

Recipe Labels and Tips

Everyone has specific needs when it comes to cooking. The recipes contain one or more of the following labels to help guide you in planning meals that fit your and your family's schedule, lifestyle, or dietary needs:

- 30 Minutes or Less
- Kid Friendly
- Family Friendly
- Gluten Free
- Dairy Free
- Vegan
- Vegetarian

BASIC INGREDIENTS

The recipes contain just five or fewer main ingredients. Italians value quality over quantity, and that's the philosophy these recipes embody. As an added benefit, many are quick to make, can be prepped in advance, and are both family friendly and guest worthy.

Most of the recipes have common, everyday ingredients that you likely already have in your kitchen. Some of these ingredients don't count toward the five unique main ingredients—they are "basics" that are called for throughout the recipes.

- salt and pepper
- olive oil
- vinegar
- fresh and dry Italian herbs
- onions and garlic
- red pepper flakes
- butter
- sugar
- all-purpose flour
- nonstick cooking spray

And since you're looking to learn more about Italian cooking and baking, why not pick up some tips as you go? These recipes are all followed by a tip in one of the following areas:

Prep Tip: How to prepare an ingredient more efficiently

Ingredient Tip: How to get the most out of an ingredient

Substitution Tip: Suggestions for alternative ingredients

Wine Pairing: A suitable wine pairing suggestion

For Your Next Visit: Names a restaurant in Italy that serves a similar dish

ANTIPASTI E CONTORNI
Appetizers and Sides

CANNELLINI CREAM WITH PARSLEY / *Crema di Cannellini con Prezzemolo* **(Tuscany)** 14

CRISPY CAULIFLOWER / *Cavolfiore Croccante* **(Trentino-Alto Adige)** 15

PROSCIUTTO-WRAPPED ASPARAGUS / *Asparagi con Prosciutto* **(Emilia-Romagna)** 17

MOZZARELLA IN A CARRIAGE / *Mozzarella in Carrozza* **(Campania)** 18

ZUCCHINI BOATS / *Barchette di Zucchine Genovese* **(Liguria)** 19

STUFFED MUSHROOMS / *Funghi Ripieni* **(Piedmont)** 20

EGGPLANT CUTLETS / *Cotolette di Melanzane* **(Sicily)** 21

GREEN BEANS IN RED SAUCE / *Fagiolini alla Pugliese* **(Puglia)** 22

PEAS WITH PANCETTA / *Piselli con Pancetta* **(Veneto)** 23

FRIED PEPPERS WITH POTATOES / *Peperoni con Potate Fritte* **(Calabria)** 24

ROMAN-STYLE SPINACH / *Spinaci alla Romana* **(Lazio)** 25

MILAN-STYLE POTATOES / *Patate in Umido alla Milanese* **(Lombardy)** 26

GRATIN-STYLE SWISS CHARD / *Bietola Gratinate* **(Calabria)** 27

PARMESAN POLENTA / *Polenta al Parmigiano* **(Valle d'Aosta)** 28

Antipasti, *Italy's version of appetizers,* are small enough to whet the appetite while leaving room for the main dish. They set the tone for the rest of the meal, and so Italians put just as much effort and care into making these starters as they do the main meal. *Contorni,* on the other hand, are side dishes generally served with the second course. Contorni border the plate, meaning they typically accompany the meat or fish that is served next to them.

CANNELLINI CREAM WITH PARSLEY
Crema di Cannellini con Prezzemolo

PREP TIME: 5 MINUTES // **COOK TIME:** NONE // **YIELD:** 1½ TO 2 CUPS OF SPREAD

Tuscans, known as *"mangia fagioli,"* or bean eaters, enjoy beans any which way they can. In the olden days, it was believed that Tuscans packed several kilos of beans when traveling abroad, so as not to go too long without eating them! Beans are favored in the winter in soups and stews, and in the summer in salads and spreads like this one. Tuscany's adoration of beans goes beyond cannellini; pinto, kidney, and great northern beans are also popular.

> 30 MINUTES OR LESS
> GLUTEN FREE
> VEGETARIAN

2 (15-ounce) cans cannellini beans, rinsed and drained

2 garlic cloves

Juice and zest of 1 lemon

Several sprigs Italian flat-leaf parsley

3 to 4 tablespoons extra-virgin olive oil

3 to 4 tablespoons grated Parmesan or Grana Padano cheese

Salt

Freshly ground black pepper

1. In a food processor or blender, combine the cannellini beans, garlic, lemon juice and zest, and parsley, and pulse until puréed.

2. Slowly drizzle in the oil while pulsing until combined.

3. Remove the blade from the food processor, and fold in the grated cheese.

4. Season with salt and pepper to taste.

5. Transfer to a serving dish. Serve with crostini, Italian bread, or fresh vegetables such as carrots or celery.

Substitution Tip: *Love chickpeas more than cannellini beans? Follow the recipe exactly as above, and substitute the cannellini beans with chickpeas.*

CRISPY CAULIFLOWER
Cavolfiore Croccante

PREP TIME: 5 MINUTES // **COOK TIME:** 25 MINUTES // **YIELD:** 4 SERVINGS

Perhaps one of the sturdiest vegetables—it can last upward of a week in the refrigerator if stored properly—cauliflower is a favorite winter vegetable for many Italians. It grows best in cold climates and doesn't much like the heat or sun, so it's not a surprise that it does best in northern Italy, where the climate is chillier. Cauliflower can be served in pasta dishes, stews, and soups; however, my preferred method is breaded and roasted in the oven.

> 30 MINUTES OR LESS
> FAMILY FRIENDLY
> VEGETARIAN

Nonstick cooking spray

1 **cauliflower**, trimmed so only the florets remain

1 teaspoon salt

1¼ cups fresh bread crumbs

½ cup freshly grated **Parmesan or Grana Padano cheese**

2 large **eggs**, slightly beaten

1. Preheat the oven to 375°F. Spray a baking sheet with cooking spray.

2. In a medium saucepan, cover the cauliflower and salt with water. Bring to a full boil and cook the florets for 4 to 5 minutes.

3. While the cauliflower is boiling, mix the bread crumbs and cheese in a medium bowl. Set aside.

4. Drain the cauliflower and rinse under cold water.

5. Dredge one floret at a time in the beaten egg, then coat in the bread crumb and cheese mixture. Place on the prepared baking sheet.

6. Bake the florets for 20 minutes, turning midway for even cooking.

Wine Pairing: *Roasted cauliflower pairs wonderfully with Italian chardonnays.*

PROSCIUTTO-WRAPPED ASPARAGUS
Asparagi con Prosciutto

PREP TIME: 5 MINUTES // **COOK TIME:** 10 TO 13 MINUTES // **YIELD:** 3 TO 4 SERVINGS

The city of Parma, in the region of Emilia-Romagna, is home to the world-famous Prosciutto di Parma. Cured only with salt and free of all additives and preservatives, this delicacy is protected by a Designation of Origin certification; DOP for short. This prosciutto is held to extremely strict curing standards, and factories are visited regularly by government agencies to ensure compliance. Although there are other prosciuttos, Prosciutto di Parma can only be produced in the province of Parma.

> 30 MINUTES OR LESS
> KID FRIENDLY
> FAMILY FRIENDLY

Nonstick cooking spray

1 bunch asparagus

2 tablespoons olive oil

2 tablespoons freshly grated Parmesan cheese

¼ pound prosciutto, cut in half lengthwise

1. Preheat the oven to 400°F, and spray a baking sheet with cooking spray.

2. Wash the asparagus and remove the bottom 1½ to 2 inches of the stalk, reserving the ends (see tip).

3. Place the asparagus spears on the baking sheet, and toss with the oil and cheese until well coated.

4. Tightly wrap a half slice of the prosciutto around the bottom half of each asparagus spear, and place on the baking sheet, prosciutto seam–down. Bake for 10 to 13 minutes, and serve immediately.

Ingredient Tip: The cut-off bottom section of the asparagus is a bit tough for roasting, but fully edible, so save it and add it to a vegetable soup or stock.

MOZZARELLA IN A CARRIAGE
Mozzarella in Carrozza

PREP TIME: 10 MINUTES // **COOK TIME:** 3 TO 4 MINUTES // **YIELD:** 2 TO 4 SERVINGS

Naples is world renowned for its mozzarella. Made from cow's milk, this semisoft cheese is a classic in countless dishes all over Naples and far beyond—including its role as the most famous pizza topping. The word *mozzarella* comes from the word "mozzare," which translates to "cutting," referring to how the curd is cut and shaped. Mozzarella in Carrozza is essentially Italy's version of a grilled cheese sandwich, only way tastier!

> 30 MINUTES OR LESS
> KID FRIENDLY
> FAMILY FRIENDLY
> VEGETARIAN

½ cup **whole milk**

2 large **eggs**

Salt

8 large **Italian bread** slices

1 large **mozzarella** ball, cut into 8 slices

Olive oil, for frying

1. In a medium bowl, whisk together the milk and eggs. Add salt to taste.

2. Using the rim of a glass, cut circles out of the bread that are about the same size as the mozzarella slices. You will need 16 circles. Reserve the extra bread fragments for another use.

3. Place a slice of mozzarella on a piece of bread and place another piece of bread on top, making a "carriage."

4. Dip both sides of the mozzarella in carrozza in the egg wash until well soaked. Place on a baking sheet, and repeat with the remaining bread and cheese.

5. In a skillet over medium heat, heat 2 to 3 inches of oil until shimmering. Working in batches, fry each mozzarella in carrozza until golden, turning once. Serve hot.

For Your Next Visit: *Headed to Italy? Be sure to try the Mozzarella in Carrozza at Perfectoo in Naples. They serve theirs with added prosciutto!*

ZUCCHINI BOATS
Barchette di Zucchine Genovese

PREP TIME: 15 MINUTES // **COOK TIME:** 25 MINUTES // **YIELD:** 4 SERVINGS

Liguria is known for stuffing just about any vegetable that's seasonably available. The most popular vegetables for stuffing include zucchini, eggplants, and bell peppers. Traditionally, vegetables were mostly stuffed with bread crumbs, grated cheese, eggs, and other ingredients most Ligurians, and all Italians, found in their kitchen. Over time, the addition of cubed salami, prosciutto, or sausage became popular.

> FAMILY FRIENDLY
> KID FRIENDLY

Nonstick cooking spray

4 medium **zucchini**

3 **pork sausages**, casings removed

½ cup **bread crumbs**

½ cup shredded **mozzarella**

½ cup freshly grated **Parmesan or Grana Padano cheese**, plus more for topping

3 tablespoons olive oil, plus more for drizzling

Salt

1. Preheat the oven to 400°F. Spray a baking dish with cooking spray.

2. Cut the zucchini lengthwise and, using a teaspoon, carefully remove some of the flesh from inside the zucchini, being careful not to break the zucchini. Finely chop the flesh and transfer it to a mixing bowl.

3. To the bowl, add the sausage, bread crumbs, mozzarella, Parmesan, and oil. Mix until well blended. Add salt to taste.

4. Spoon the mixture into the zucchini boats and place them on the prepared baking dish. Sprinkle additional grated cheese and drizzle additional oil on top.

5. Bake for 25 minutes.

Substitution Tip: *Chicken or turkey sausages can be used in place of the pork sausages.*

STUFFED MUSHROOMS
Funghi Ripieni

PREP TIME: 10 MINUTES // **COOK TIME:** 20 MINUTES // **YIELD:** 4 SERVINGS

Mushrooms filled with their own stems, bread crumbs, grated cheese, and herbs set the stage for a promising meal ahead. Stuffing is by far the preferred method of cooking *funghi champignon,* or what we know in the United States as white button mushrooms. Many believe that the best ones are grown in Piedmont. Easy to recognize and mild in flavor when compared to other varieties of mushroom, funghi champignon are inexpensive and adaptable, and also make a welcome addition to soups or gravies.

> 30 MINUTES OR LESS
> FAMILY FRIENDLY
> VEGETARIAN

Nonstick cooking spray

12 large white stuffing mushrooms, cleaned and stems removed and reserved

2 garlic cloves, finely chopped

2 tablespoons chopped fresh parsley

4 tablespoons olive oil

¾ cup bread crumbs, plus extra for topping

½ cup grated Parmesan cheese, plus extra for topping

Salt

1. Preheat the oven to 400°F. Spray a baking sheet with cooking spray.

2. Finely chop the mushroom stems and place them in a mixing bowl. Add the garlic, parsley, oil, bread crumbs, Parmesan cheese, and salt. Mix all the ingredients well. The mixture should be moist, so add another drizzle of oil if needed.

3. Salt the inside of the mushroom caps and stuff the caps with the stuffing. Place the mushroom caps on the baking sheet and sprinkle the tops with a pinch of bread crumbs and Parmesan cheese. Bake for 20 minutes.

Prep tip: These mushrooms can be prepared up to 6 hours in advance, so if you are having friends for dinner, prep them in the morning and refrigerate until it's time to bake them.

EGGPLANT CUTLETS
Cotolette di Melanzane

PREP TIME: 15 MINUTES // **COOK TIME:** 10 MINUTES // **YIELD:** 4 TO 6 SERVINGS

Eggplant is a favorite, especially in the regions of Sicily and Calabria, where the constant sunshine makes it ideal for growing. Whether you choose to peel the eggplant or not is entirely up to you.

> 30 MINUTES OR LESS
> KID FRIENDLY
> FAMILY FRIENDLY
> VEGETARIAN

2 large eggplants, cut into
   ¼-inch slices
Salt
1 cup fresh bread crumbs
½ cup freshly grated
   Parmesan cheese
1 cup all-purpose flour
2 eggs, beaten
Vegetable oil, for frying

1. Salt both sides of the eggplant slices and allow to rest on paper towels for 5 minutes.

2. In a shallow dish, combine the bread crumbs and Parmesan cheese and blend well. Pour the flour into a separate dish.

3. Lightly dredge each eggplant slice in the flour, shaking off the excess. Dip each slice in the beaten eggs, then dredge in the bread crumb and cheese mixture. Set aside on a baking sheet.

4. In a large frying pan over medium-high heat, heat about 1 inch of oil until shimmering. Working in batches, add a few slices of eggplant. Cook until lightly browned, about 2 minutes per side. If browning too quickly, lower the heat. Transfer the browned cutlets to paper towels and continue with the rest of the slices.

5. Plate and serve hot.

Substitution Tip: Not a fan of eggplant? No problem—you can use the same exact method for preparing zucchini cutlets.

GREEN BEANS IN RED SAUCE
Fagiolini alla Pugliese

PREP TIME: 10 MINUTES // **COOK TIME:** 25 MINUTES // **YIELD:** 4 SERVINGS

If there's one dish I most recall eating on summer days while growing up in Italy, it's green beans in red sauce. It wasn't until years later that I learned that this dish is a specialty of Puglia. Clearly, my home region of Calabria has been influenced by our neighbor. The people of Puglia enjoy an abundance of produce; they prepare this as a side, or add some pasta and serve it as a first course.

> GLUTEN FREE
> DAIRY FREE
> VEGAN
> VEGETARIAN

2 pounds fresh green beans, ends trimmed

3 tablespoons olive oil

2 garlic cloves, minced

2½ cups ground peeled tomatoes

2 tablespoons chopped fresh parsley, plus more for garnish

1. Bring a large pot of salted water to a full boil. Boil the green beans for 15 to 20 minutes until almost cooked.

2. In the meantime, prepare the sauce. In a large skillet over medium heat, simmer the oil and garlic for a few minutes until the garlic is fragrant. Add the tomatoes and parsley and cook for 10 minutes.

3. Drain the green beans and add them to the sauce. Cook the beans in the sauce for a few minutes, mixing well so the beans are well coated. Sprinkle with chopped parsley and serve.

Substitution Tip: If fresh green beans are out of season, you can substitute with high-quality frozen green beans; however, canned beans are not recommended. Adjust the cooking time, as they will require less boiling.

PEAS WITH PANCETTA
Piselli con Pancetta

PREP TIME: 5 MINUTES // **COOK TIME:** 20 MINUTES // **YIELD:** 4 TO 6 SERVINGS

Adored by young and old from northern to southern Italy, peas with pancetta is a favorite side dish for many Italians, especially in the Veneto region. Peas are so highly regarded in this northern area of Italy that the city of Vicenza holds a two-day festival dedicated to this beloved vegetable not once, but twice a year. Economical and quick, peas with pancetta make a great side for chicken or meat.

> 30 MINUTES OR LESS
> KID FRIENDLY
> FAMILY FRIENDLY
> GLUTEN FREE
> DAIRY FREE

1 small onion, chopped

½ teaspoon salt

3 tablespoons olive oil

3 ounces pancetta, diced

1 pound frozen peas

1 cup Quick Vegetable Broth (page 39) or water

1. In a large sauté pan over medium heat, simmer the onion, salt, and oil for about 3 minutes.

2. Add the pancetta and allow the fat to render. Brown for several minutes longer.

3. Add the peas and broth, reduce the heat to medium-low, and simmer for 20 minutes. If the peas begin to dry out, add an additional ½ cup of water.

For Your Next Visit: *If you're headed to Veneto in May, be sure to check out the Sagra dei Bisi or Festival of Peas in Lumigano di Longare province of Vicenza. While always held in May, peak season for fresh peas, the exact dates change from year to year, so be sure to check the date before planning.*

FRIED PEPPERS WITH POTATOES
Peperoni con Potate Fritte

PREP TIME: 15 MINUTES // **COOK TIME:** 20 MINUTES // **YIELD:** 4 TO 5 SERVINGS

If there is one dish that screams Calabria, it's fried peppers and potatoes. Enjoyed throughout the year, this peasant dish comprised of just a few basic ingredients is frequently served as a side dish to meat and fish, as well as in sub rolls for a vegetarian panino. Calabrians adore this dish because the main ingredients are inexpensive, and peppers grow so easily under the southern Italian sun.

> 30 MINUTES OR LESS
> KID FRIENDLY
> FAMILY FRIENDLY
> GLUTEN FREE
> DAIRY FREE
> VEGAN
> VEGETARIAN

⅓ cup olive oil

3 or 4 large bell peppers of mixed colors, cut into strips

3 medium potatoes, peeled and cut into ¼-inch strips

1 medium onion, thinly sliced

1 teaspoon salt

1 teaspoon dried oregano

1 tablespoon chopped fresh parsley

1. In a large skillet or sauté pan over medium-high heat, heat the oil. Add the peppers, potatoes, onion, salt, oregano, and parsley, stirring to combine.

2. Reduce the heat to medium and mix all the ingredients well, paying close attention that the potatoes do not stick to the pan (see tip). Adjust the heat accordingly.

3. Continue frying the peppers and potatoes, stirring frequently, until fully cooked, about 20 minutes. Add additional oil if necessary. Serve hot.

Ingredient Tip: *Potatoes have a tendency to stick, even in nonstick frying pans. If you notice that they are sticking to the pan, reduce the heat and add a few more tablespoons of oil.*

ROMAN-STYLE SPINACH
Spinaci alla Romana

PREP TIME: 5 MINUTES, PLUS INACTIVE TIME // **COOK TIME:** 10 MINUTES // **YIELD:** 4 SERVINGS

Roman spinach is a family favorite for home cooks, as well as a side dish frequently found on restaurant menus. Pine nuts are a favorite ingredient for Romans; in fact, the city is filled with pine nut trees that provide shade as well as this delicious nut.

> 30 MINUTES OR LESS
> FAMILY FRIENDLY
> VEGETARIAN

½ cup **raisins**
1 pound **spinach**
2 tablespoons butter
Salt
½ cup **pine nuts**

1. Soak the raisins for 15 minutes in hot water.

2. Meanwhile, wash the spinach and trim any large or thick ends. Thinner stems can be left untrimmed as they will easily cook down.

3. In a skillet or sauté pan over medium heat, melt the butter. Add the spinach and salt to taste, cover, and allow the spinach to wilt down for several minutes.

4. Meanwhile, drain the raisins well, squeezing out any extra water.

5. Add the raisins and pine nuts to the spinach. Stir and cook together for several minutes longer until all the flavors are well incorporated.

Substitution Tip: Frozen spinach, often more economical, can be substituted in this recipe. Be sure to thaw it fully and squeeze out any excess water before adding it to the melted butter.

MILAN-STYLE POTATOES
Patate in Umido alla Milanese

PREP TIME: 15 MINUTES // **COOK TIME:** 25 MINUTES // **YIELD:** 4 SERVINGS

Potatoes are hardly regional in Italy; they are enjoyed throughout the country. One of the least seasonal vegetables, potatoes are found readily throughout the entire year. They are perhaps the most versatile vegetable to boot. As a result, it is estimated that Italians eat upward of 80 kilos of potatoes a year—that's about 175 pounds! In Milan, people prefer serving potatoes in red sauce, or *umido*. Mostly a homestyle dish, potatoes in red sauce taste especially wonderful in the cold winter months.

> FAMILY FRIENDLY
> GLUTEN FREE

1½ to 2 pounds potatoes
2 tablespoons butter
1 small onion, diced
¼ cup diced pancetta
1½ cups ground
   peeled tomatoes
½ cup cold water
1 teaspoon salt
1 tablespoon chopped
   fresh parsley

1. Peel the potatoes, rinse them under cold water, and carefully slice them into circles resembling thick potato chips, about ⅛-inch thick. Set aside.

2. In a large sauté pan over medium heat, melt the butter, add the onion, and simmer for several minutes. Add the pancetta and allow the fat to render. Cook for 4 to 5 minutes.

3. Add the potatoes and cook for several minutes to lightly brown them.

4. Add the tomatoes, water, and salt. Reduce the heat to low and simmer for 20 minutes, stirring occasionally. Add the chopped parsley before serving.

For Your Next Visit: *If you are headed to Milan, be sure to visit Gialle & Co., the only restaurant that focuses solely on potatoes!*

GRATIN-STYLE SWISS CHARD
Bietola Gratinate

PREP TIME: 15 MINUTES // **COOK TIME:** 13 MINUTES // **YIELD:** 4 SERVINGS

A favorite of Calabria, Swiss chard is a common side dish in the summer months, its prime growing season. Whether served as a side, added to frittatas, or even fried in patties or fritters, Swiss chard is economical and a main staple of Calabria's *"cucina povera,"* or poor man's cooking. At one time it was simply served with a drizzle of extra-virgin olive oil, but adding more expensive ingredients such as Parmesan is now a common practice.

> 30 MINUTES OR LESS
> VEGETARIAN

Salt

2 large bunches Swiss chard, washed and cut into 1-inch pieces

3 tablespoons olive oil

½ cup bread crumbs, plus 2 tablespoons, divided

¼ cup grated Parmesan cheese

1. Bring a large stockpot of salted water to a boil. Add the Swiss chard to the boiling water and cook for 10 minutes.

2. Drain the Swiss chard and place it in a large sauté pan. Add the oil and ½ cup of bread crumbs to the pan. Cook over medium heat for 2 minutes, mixing well.

3. Remove from the heat and add the grated Parmesan cheese. Mix well so the cheese melts fully. Add the 2 remaining tablespoons of bread crumbs and mix well. Serve immediately.

Prep Tip: If you're prepping a large meal and want to get a head start, you can boil the Swiss chard up to 8 hours before, refrigerate it, and complete the sauté steps right before serving.

PARMESAN POLENTA
Polenta al Parmigiano

PREP TIME: 5 MINUTES // **COOK TIME:** 15 MINUTES // **YIELD:** 4 TO 6 SERVINGS

While eaten throughout the entire country, polenta is most appreciated and enjoyed in northern Italy, as it makes for a warming dish in the cooler regions. Paired with red sauces, boar, or mushrooms, or very often eaten alone, polenta can be served as an alternative to mashed potatoes.

> 30 MINUTES OR LESS
> FAMILY FRIENDLY
> VEGETARIAN

5 cups water or Quick Vegetable Broth (page 39)

1 teaspoon salt

1½ cups instant polenta (also known in the United States as cornmeal)

½ cup grated Parmesan cheese

2 tablespoons butter

¼ teaspoon grated nutmeg (optional)

1. In a medium saucepan, bring the water to a boil and add the salt.

2. Reduce the heat to medium and add the polenta in a very slow stream, whisking continuously so it does not stick to the pan.

3. Continue stirring until the polenta thickens and begins to pull from the side of the pan, 10 to 15 minutes for instant polenta.

4. Remove from the heat and add the grated cheese, butter, and nutmeg. Mix until the butter and cheese are melted. Serve immediately.

Wine Pairing: *Polenta goes very well with red wines, so enjoy this contorno with a glass of Barbera or Cabernet.*

3

ZUPPE E INSALATE
Soups and Salads

REINFORCEMENT SALAD / *Insalata di Rinforzo* **(Campania)** 32

TOMATO, POTATO, AND EGG SALAD / *Insalata di Pomodori, Patate, e Uova* **(Calabria)** 33

SICILIAN SALAD / *Insalata Pantesca* **(Sicily)** 35

ORANGE AND RED ONION SALAD / *Insalata di Arance e Cipolle Rosse* **(Sicily)** 36

CAPRESE SALAD / *Insalata Caprese* **(Campania)** 37

BEAN AND TUNA SALAD / *Insalata di Tonno e Cannellini* **(Southern Italy)** 38

QUICK VEGETABLE BROTH / *Brodo Vegetariano* **(Italy)** 39

SAVOY CABBAGE AND BEANS SOUP / *Zuppa di Verza e Fagioli* **(Veneto)** 40

CHICKPEA SOUP / *Zuppa di Cicerchia* **(Marche)** 41

TUSCAN BEAN SOUP / *Minestra di Cannellini* **(Tuscany)** 43

LENTIL SOUP / *Minestra di Lenticchie* **(Tuscany)** 44

TORTELLINI IN BROTH / *Tortellini en Brodo* **(Emilia-Romagna)** 45

Warming, comforting, and gratifying, soups are what Italian winters are made for. Be it with legumes in the Tuscany region or some tortellini soup in Emilia-Romagna, *zuppe* can be part of a larger meal or a main meal itself.

Italy has a large repertoire of *insalate*, or salads. But there is far more to salads than leafy greens. Salads vary greatly between regions and consist of local ingredients. Light salads can often start or end a meal, while heavier salads may be served as a light meal alone, with perhaps a small piece of bread on the side.

REINFORCEMENT SALAD
Insalata di Rinforzo

PREP TIME: 20 MINUTES, PLUS INACTIVE TIME // **COOK TIME:** 5 TO 6 MINUTES // **YIELD:** 4 SERVINGS

It would be rare to find a household in Naples not enjoying this salad during Christmas Eve dinner. The specific origin of the name is unknown, but it is believed that it comes from the ability to "reinforce" this salad with fresh ingredients so it can be enjoyed throughout the holiday week between Christmas and New Year's. While the actual ingredients vary in every household, some of the main ingredients include cauliflower, pickled vegetables, and vinegar.

> 30 MINUTES OR LESS
> FAMILY FRIENDLY
> GLUTEN FREE
> DAIRY FREE
> VEGAN
> VEGETARIAN

Salt

1 head **cauliflower**, separated into small florets

3 **carrots**, peeled and cut into ½-inch pieces

½ cup **mixed olives**, pitted

2 to 3 tablespoons **capers**

1 cup **white wine vinegar**

3 tablespoons extra-virgin olive oil

Freshly ground black pepper

1. In a pot of salted water, boil the cauliflower florets and carrots for 4 to 5 minutes.

2. Drain the vegetables, rinse them under cold water, and transfer to a large salad bowl.

3. To the bowl, add the olives, capers, vinegar, and oil. Mix well so all the flavors are incorporated. Add salt and pepper to taste.

4. For the best flavor, allow the salad to sit for at least 4 hours at room temperature. For longer storage, refrigerate in an airtight glass container.

Substitution Tip: While cauliflower is a staple in this salad, the other ingredients are only limited by your imagination. Some other options could include bell peppers, celery, pickling onions or regular onions, fennel, garlic, and anchovies.

TOMATO, POTATO, AND EGG SALAD
Insalata di Pomodori, Patate, e Uova

PREP TIME: 10 MINUTES // **COOK TIME:** 20 MINUTES // **YIELD:** 4 TO 6 SERVINGS

Often served in the summer months when tomatoes are at their peak, this salad is a staple in Calabria. With locally grown tomatoes and local olive oil, this salad can be a lunch or dinner option, especially during the summer when cooking a larger meal over a hot stove is too laborious. This salad uses a lot of oil, as the potatoes soak it up like a sponge.

> 30 MINUTES OR LESS
> KID FRIENDLY
> FAMILY FRIENDLY
> GLUTEN FREE
> DAIRY FREE
> VEGETARIAN

2 pounds medium **potatoes**

6 large **eggs**

3 medium **vine-ripened tomatoes**

¼ cup extra-virgin olive oil

Salt

1 teaspoon dried oregano

2 tablespoons chopped fresh basil

1. In a large stockpot halfway filled with cold water, bring the unpeeled potatoes and eggs to a boil, and boil for about 20 minutes or until the potatoes are fork-tender.

2. Meanwhile, cut the tomatoes into 1-inch pieces. Put them in a large salad bowl. Add the oil and season with salt, tossing to coat.

3. Peel the potatoes and dice them into 1-inch pieces. Peel the eggs, quarter them, and then cut them again into three or four smaller pieces.

4. Add the potatoes and eggs to the tomatoes. Mix well and stir in the oregano and basil. Add additional oil as needed. Serve immediately while still warm.

Wine Pairing: *Eggs pair nicely with sauvignon blanc, so grab an Italian bottle to go with this summery salad.*

SICILIAN SALAD
Insalata Pantesca

PREP TIME: 15 MINUTES // **COOK TIME:** 15 MINUTES // **YIELD:** 2 TO 4 SERVINGS

Tomatoes, capers, and red onions—these are some of the major flavors of Sicily. This salad brings all these ingredients together nicely in an easy summer salad that delivers a strong, robust flavor. Originating from the island of Pantelleria, a renowned area for producing capers, this salad sometimes contains tuna canned in oil, mackerel, anchovies, or black olives.

> 30 MINUTES OR LESS
> GLUTEN FREE
> DAIRY FREE
> VEGAN
> VEGETARIAN

2 or 3 medium **potatoes**

4 medium **vine-ripened plum tomatoes**

1 small red onion, thinly sliced

1 tablespoon **capers**, rinsed

3 tablespoons chopped fresh basil

3 tablespoons extra-virgin olive oil

¼ teaspoon salt, or more or less as desired

1. Put the unpeeled potatoes in a medium saucepan with enough water to cover them, and boil until fork tender, 15 to 20 minutes.

2. Meanwhile, dice the tomatoes into 1-inch cubes and put them in a salad bowl. Add the red onion, capers, basil, oil, and salt, and mix well.

3. Drain the cooked potatoes and quickly rinse under cold water to cool slightly. Peel and dice or slice the potatoes according to your preference. Add the potatoes to the bowl with the tomatoes. Mix well so all the flavors develop. Serve as a salad or light first course.

For Your Next Visit: *Headed to Sicily? Be sure to stop by the Sagra Del Cappero, or festival of the caper. This feast, devoted to this distinguished flower bud, is celebrated the first Sunday in June in Salina.*

ORANGE AND RED ONION SALAD
Insalata di Arance e Cipolle Rosse

PREP TIME: 15 MINUTES // **COOK TIME:** NONE // **YIELD:** 4 SERVINGS

Kissed by the sun year round, Sicily is famous for its oranges and other citrus fruits; in fact, it's the region where most citrus are grown. While at first these ingredients might not seem to go very well together, put your doubts aside and see that they actually offer a refreshing alternative to everyday salads.

> 30 MINUTES OR LESS
> GLUTEN FREE
> DAIRY FREE
> VEGAN
> VEGETARIAN

3 or 4 tablespoons extra-virgin olive oil

Juice of 1 lemon

Salt

Freshly ground black pepper

4 large oranges

1 large red onion, thinly sliced

¼ cup olives of choice, pitted

1. Prepare the vinaigrette by combining the oil, lemon juice, and salt and pepper to taste in a small bowl. Mix well with a fork and set aside.

2. Thoroughly peel the oranges and remove all the white pith. Cut the oranges into ⅛-inch-thick slices and decoratively arrange the fruit on a platter.

3. Top the oranges with thin slices of red onion and sprinkle with the olives.

4. Dress the salad with the prepared vinaigrette. Season with additional salt and pepper, if desired.

Substitution Tip: If you happen to have grapefruits on hand as opposed to oranges, feel free to substitute. Any citrus fruit will do for this citrus salad.

CAPRESE SALAD
Insalata Caprese

PREP TIME: 5 MINUTES // **COOK TIME:** NONE // **YIELD:** 2 TO 4 SERVINGS

Originating from the island of Capri, this salad is a wonderful example of how just a few high-quality ingredients can create something magical. Believed to be a fairly new creation by Italian standards, the story goes that in the mid-1950s, a patriotic resident of Capri wanted to create a dish that symbolized Italy and the Italian flag.

> 30 MINUTES OR LESS
> FAMILY FRIENDLY
> VEGETARIAN

1 large **beefsteak or vine-ripened tomato**

1 (6- to 8-ounce) ball fresh **mozzarella** (see tip)

About 10 basil leaves

1 to 2 tablespoons extra-virgin olive oil

Salt

1. Slice the tomato into ¼-inch-thick slices and arrange on a platter in a wide circle.

2. Slice the mozzarella to about the same size as the tomato, and arrange on top of the tomato, alternating layers so the tomato and mozzarella overlap.

3. Arrange the basil in between the tomato and mozzarella so they overlap.

4. Drizzle with the olive oil and salt to taste.

Ingredient Tip: Fresh mozzarella should be stored in the water it came in, used within a few days of purchase, be free of any odor, and appear purely white, with no sign of discoloration.

Wine Pairing: Choose a wine that is high in acid to complement the acid in the tomatoes. A Soave or sauvignon blanc will pair nicely with this crisp salad.

BEAN AND TUNA SALAD
Insalata di Tonno e Cannellini

PREP TIME: 10 MINUTES // **COOK TIME:** NONE // **YIELD:** 4 SERVINGS

Economical, easy, and very flavorful, this salad combines a few quick ingredients to yield a delicious salad or light summer lunch. Eaten all over Italy, particularly in the south, this salad contains fiber, protein, and heart-healthy olive oil. Tuna packed in oil adds great flavor; some trusted brands I use include Genova and Cento. Bumble Bee also makes oil-packed tuna that is available at most grocery stores.

> 30 MINUTES OR LESS
> GLUTEN FREE
> DAIRY FREE

2 (15-ounce) cans **cannellini beans**, rinsed and drained

½ small onion, thinly sliced

2 (5-ounce) cans **solid tuna packed in oil**

1 tablespoon chopped fresh basil or parsley

Extra-virgin olive oil

Juice of ½ **lemon**

½ teaspoon salt

1. In a medium salad bowl, combine the beans and onion.

2. In a separate small bowl, break the tuna up into small pieces. Add the tuna and the oil it came with into the bowl with the beans.

3. Add the basil or parsley, olive oil as needed, lemon juice, and salt. Mix well and serve immediately.

Ingredient Tip: *If you happen to have olives, capers, or anchovies on hand, feel free to add them to this salad. These flavors work very well together and will take this dish to another level.*

QUICK VEGETABLE BROTH
Brodo Vegetariano

PREP TIME: 10 MINUTES // **COOK TIME:** 1 HOUR // **YIELD:** 6 CUPS OF BROTH

While not solely an Italian staple, a good vegetarian broth will add depth of flavor to many Italian dishes such as soups and risottos. It really only takes a few minutes to prepare and requires no attention as it simmers, not even stirring! This is a basic recipe that can be altered as you like. Other vegetables you can add include leeks, fennel, asparagus, turnips, and peas. Avoid potatoes, as they tend to break down and cloud up the broth.

> GLUTEN FREE
> DAIRY FREE
> VEGAN
> VEGETARIAN

2 tablespoons olive oil

2 large onions, chopped

4 celery stalks, chopped

4 carrots, chopped

1 (8-ounce) can
   crushed tomatoes

8 cups cold water

2 bay leaves

Fresh parsley sprigs

Salt

Freshly ground black pepper

1. In a large stockpot over medium heat, combine the oil, onions, celery, carrots, and tomatoes. Cook, stirring frequently, until the vegetables are softened, 7 to 8 minutes.

2. Add the water, bay leaves, parsley, salt, and pepper. Reduce the heat to low and simmer for 45 minutes to 1 hour.

3. Strain the broth, discarding the vegetables. The broth can be refrigerated for up to 4 days or frozen for later use.

Ingredient Tip: *This broth is a wonderful base for cooking pastina. You don't have to strain the vegetables; just add some small-cut pasta for a light first course.*

SAVOY CABBAGE AND BEANS SOUP
Zuppa di Verza e Fagioli

PREP TIME: 15 MINUTES // **COOK TIME:** 25 TO 30 MINUTES // **YIELD:** 4 SERVINGS

A favorite of Veneto, this wintry soup is prepared with a few very inexpensive and humble ingredients—savoy cabbage and canned beans—but it's enriched by adding a few more costly and flavorful elements, such as Parmesan cheese and pancetta. Savory and warming, this soup makes a great first course or full meal in itself.

> 30 MINUTES OR LESS
> FAMILY FRIENDLY

½ medium **savoy cabbage**, about 2 pounds

3 to 4 tablespoons olive oil

¼ cup **pancetta** cubes

1 small onion, finely chopped

2 (15-ounce) cans **cannellini beans**, rinsed and drained

6 cups **Quick Vegetable Broth** (page 39), or 1 vegetable bouillon cube dissolved in 6 cups boiling water

4 tablespoons grated **Parmesan cheese**, for topping

1. Clean the cabbage by discarding the outer few leaves, and give it a rough chop. Rinse and set aside.

2. In a large soup pot over medium heat, combine the oil, pancetta, and onion, and simmer for several minutes until browned and the fat in the pancetta has rendered.

3. Add the beans, chopped cabbage, and vegetable broth. Bring the soup to a full boil and cook until the cabbage is tender, about 20 minutes.

4. Top each serving with 1 tablespoon of Parmesan cheese.

Prep Tip: To save time, you can chop the cabbage well in advance of preparing the soup. If desired, pre-boil the cabbage until almost cooked, and then prepare the soup. Adjust cooking time accordingly.

CHICKPEA SOUP
Zuppa di Cicerchia

PREP TIME: 10 MINUTES // **COOK TIME:** 20 MINUTES // **YIELD:** 4 SERVINGS

A typical ingredient and the culinary symbol of the Marche region, *cicerchia* is a legume very much resembling what we know as chickpeas. Served mostly in the cold winter months, this satisfying dish is nutritious and filling. Pair it with some toasted bread and an additional drizzle of olive oil to make it a complete light meal.

> 30 MINUTES OR LESS
> DAIRY FREE
> VEGAN
> VEGETARIAN

3 tablespoons olive oil, plus more for drizzling

½ small onion, chopped

2 carrots, peeled and finely diced

1 (14-ounce) can diced tomatoes

4 cups Quick Vegetable Broth (page 39), or ½ large bouillon cube dissolved in 4 cups boiling water

2 cans chickpeas, drained and rinsed

12 ounces fresh spinach

Salt

Freshly ground black pepper

1. In a large stockpot, heat the oil over medium heat.

2. Add the onion and carrots, and sauté for several minutes until the vegetables soften slightly. Add the tomatoes.

3. Add the broth and enough water to fill the pan a bit past the halfway mark. Bring the soup to a full boil.

4. Once the broth is boiling, add the chickpeas and spinach, and simmer for 15 minutes.

5. Add salt and pepper to taste and drizzle with additional oil, if desired.

Substitution Tip: *In place of the spinach, you can use Swiss chard, escarole, cabbage, or any other leafy green.*

TUSCAN BEAN SOUP
Minestra di Cannellini

PREP TIME: 10 MINUTES // **COOK TIME:** 25 MINUTES // **YIELD:** 4 SERVINGS

It's very common in Italy to add pork products to soups, especially soups containing legumes. Sausages, pork shank, pancetta, or pork bits are just a few of the options. For ease of cooking and efficiency, we use pork sausages in this recipe. This soup refrigerates well and is as delicious served the next day as it is the day it's prepared.

> FAMILY FRIENDLY

3 tablespoons olive oil

2 carrots, peeled and diced

1 small onion, diced

3 tablespoons chopped fresh parsley

3 hot Italian sausages, cut into 4 or 5 pieces

1 (8-ounce) can diced tomatoes

2 (15-ounce) cans cannellini beans, rinsed and drained

Salt

1. In a large soup pot, combine the oil, carrots, onion, and parsley. Sauté for 2 to 3 minutes until they have taken on some color but are still a bit crunchy. Add the sausage and, mixing with a wooden spoon, brown it on all sides for 2 to 3 minutes.

2. Add the tomatoes and continue sautéing for 2 to 3 minutes longer. Add the beans and enough water to cover all the ingredients. Add salt to taste.

3. Bring to a boil, and continue boiling for an additional 20 minutes or until the beans are fully cooked.

Prep Tip: *Ingredients such as carrots, celery, onions, and parsley are used in many soups and stews. Chop a good amount of each when you have a few spare minutes. Once refrigerated, you can just grab what you need when you're ready to cook!*

LENTIL SOUP
Minestra di Lenticchie

PREP TIME: 10 MINUTES, PLUS INACTIVE TIME // **COOK TIME:** 30 MINUTES // **YIELD:** 4 SERVINGS

Eaten all over Italy, particularly in northern Italy, lentils have a nutty flavor, are economical, and contain lots of protein and fiber. Believed to resemble little coins, lentils are enjoyed by Italians on New Year's Day as an omen for prosperity in the year ahead.

> GLUTEN FREE
> DAIRY FREE
> VEGAN
> VEGETARIAN

1 cup dried lentils

1 small onion, finely diced

2 tablespoons chopped fresh parsley

2 or 3 carrots, peeled and thinly sliced

1 celery stalk, thinly sliced

3 tablespoons olive oil

1 teaspoon salt

1 (8-ounce) can tomatoes

3 cups Quick Vegetable Broth (page 39), or ½ large bouillon cube dissolved in 3 cups boiling water

Water

1. In a large bowl filled with cold water, soak the lentils for 1 hour.

2. In a large soup pot over medium-low heat, combine the onion, parsley, carrots, celery, oil, and salt, and sauté for several minutes until they become golden and fragrant.

3. Add the tomatoes and simmer for an additional minute.

4. Add the lentils, broth, and enough water to fully cover all the ingredients.

5. Simmer the soup over medium heat for 20 to 25 minutes until the lentils are fully cooked.

Prep Tip: Although lentils don't require soaking, they will cook faster if soaked in cold water for at least 1 hour.

TORTELLINI IN BROTH
Tortellini en Brodo

PREP TIME: 10 MINUTES // **COOK TIME:** 20 MINUTES // **YIELD:** 3 TO 4 SERVINGS

If there is one dish in the cities of Modena and Bologna that screams authenticity, it must be tortellini. Filled with cheeses, meats, or a combination thereof, this stuffed pasta is a favorite in cities and beyond and is served at home as frequently as it is in restaurants. Most often prepared in chicken, beef, or vegetable *brodo* (broth), this delicately rich soup is a favorite of kids and adults alike.

> 30 MINUTES OR LESS
> KID FRIENDLY
> FAMILY FRIENDLY

2 **carrots**, peeled and diced

2 **celery stalks**, diced

1 small onion, diced

1 tablespoon chopped fresh parsley

2 tablespoons olive oil

1 teaspoon salt

6 cups **Quick Vegetable Broth** (page 39)

1 (9- to 12-ounce) package **fresh tortellini** (such as Buitoni)

Grated **Parmesan cheese**, for topping

1. In a medium soup pot, combine the carrots, celery, onion, parsley, oil, salt, and broth, and bring to a full boil. Allow the soup to boil for 15 minutes to build flavor.

2. Add the fresh tortellini and cook it according to the package instructions. Fresh pasta cooks very fast, so pay close attention to not overcook or the tortellini will break apart.

3. Plate and sprinkle with grated Parmesan before serving.

For Your Next Visit: *Headed to Bologna? Be sure to try the tortellini at Bottega Portici, located on Via dell'Indipendenza.*

RISOTTO, PASTA, E SALSE
Risotto, Pasta, and Sauces

BASIC TOMATO SAUCE / *Sugo di Pomodoro* **(Italy)** 48

BECHAMEL CREAM / *Crema di Besciamella* **(Emilia-Romagna)** 49

BASIL PESTO / *Pesto alla Genovese* **(Liguria)** 50

SICILIAN PESTO / *Pesto Siciliano* **(Sicily)** 51

BASIC WHITE RISOTTO / *Risotto Bianco* **(Lombardy)** 52

RICE WITH PEAS / *Risi e Bisi* **(Veneto)** 53

HOMEMADE PASTA / *Pasta Fatta in Casa* **(Emilia-Romagna)** 54

PASTA WITH BREAD CRUMBS / *Fusilli alla Mollica* **(Basilicata)** 56

LITTLE EARS WITH BROCCOLI RABE AND SAUSAGE /
Orecchiette con Cime di Rapa e Salsiccia **(Puglia)** 57

SPAGHETTI WITH CLAM SAUCE / *Spaghetti con Vongole* **(Abbruzzo)** 58

AMATRICIANA-STYLE BUCATINI / *Bucatini all'Amatriciana* **(Lazio)** 59

ANGRY PENNE / *Penne Arrabbiata* **(Lazio and Campania)** 60

PASTA WITH CANNELLINI BEANS / *Pasta e Fagioli* **(Friuli-Venezia Giulia)** 61

NORCINA-STYLE PASTA / *Pasta alla Norcina* **(Umbria)** 62

PASTA CARBONARA / *Pasta alla Carbonara* **(Lazio)** 63

PASTA WITH GARLIC AND OLIVE OIL / *Pasta Aglio e Olio* **(Campania)** 64

For Italians, a day without pasta is a day wasted! Served mostly as a first course, after the antipasto and before the second course of meat or fish, rice and pasta are imperative to Italian cuisine—perhaps more so than any other food or course. For ease, most of the recipes in this chapter call for dry pasta, but because nothing compares to fresh pasta, I've included a recipe for Homemade Pasta (page 54). It's simple, basic, and all purpose.

How one adorns the pasta or rice is as important as the pasta itself, whether that means stirring it with fancy red or white sauces or topping it with fish or vegetables. With thousands of pasta shapes available and equally as many ways to prepare it, when it comes to pasta, you are only limited by your imagination.

BASIC TOMATO SAUCE
Sugo di Pomodoro

PREP TIME: 5 MINUTES // **COOK TIME:** 25 MINUTES // **YIELD:** 3 TO 4 CUPS

One of the most basic and best-received recipes I teach in my Italian cooking classes is this simple, yet surprisingly delicious, tomato sauce. It's predominantly used to make *pasta al pomodoro*; however, this versatile sauce is a mainstay in many dishes, including soups, stews, pizzas, and baked pasta dishes.

> 30 MINUTES OR LESS
> KID FRIENDLY
> FAMILY FRIENDLY
> DAIRY FREE
> VEGAN
> VEGETARIAN

3 tablespoons olive oil

½ small onion, finely diced

2 tablespoons chopped
fresh parsley

2 or 3 garlic cloves,
finely chopped

1 (28-ounce) can high-quality
crushed tomatoes
(see Choosing Quality
Ingredients, page 5)

1 cup water

½ teaspoon salt

3 to 5 fresh basil leaves

1. In a medium saucepan over medium-low heat, heat the oil for 1 minute. Add the onion and parsley. Once the onion is translucent, about 2 minutes, add the garlic and cook for 1 minute more.

2. Carefully add the tomatoes; they will splatter as they hit the hot oil. Add the water, salt, and basil leaves. Reduce the heat to low, cover, and let simmer for 20 minutes.

Prep Tip: *This basic tomato sauce freezes really well, and it's very convenient to make some in advance to freeze. Divide into small cup-size containers and freeze until ready to use. Thaw overnight in the refrigerator or as needed in the microwave.*

BECHAMEL CREAM
Crema di Besciamella

PREP TIME: 5 MINUTES // **COOK TIME:** 15 MINUTES // **YIELD:** 2 CUPS

A basic white sauce that should be in everyone's culinary repertoire, béchamel is believed to be primarily a French sauce, although rumor has it that an Italian chef first created this while in France. This sauce is a base for most lasagna dishes in northern Italy and is frequently added to red sauces as a way to enrich them—it's also popular with kids. Simply add some small, fun-shaped pasta to this sauce, and you have a children's favorite.

> 30 MINUTES OR LESS
> KID FRIENDLY
> FAMILY FRIENDLY
> VEGETARIAN

2 cups **whole milk**
3 tablespoons butter
4 tablespoons flour
Salt
Grated **nutmeg** (optional)

1. In a small saucepan, heat the milk to almost boiling.

2. Meanwhile, in a larger saucepan over low heat, melt the butter. Sift the flour over the butter and, using a wire whisk, mix well until the mixture is smooth. Continue cooking the flour and butter for one minute, paying close attention so that the mixture does not brown.

3. Slowly pour the hot milk into the flour and butter mixture, stirring constantly. The cream will be thick at first but will loosen up as the milk is added.

4. Add salt to taste and continue whisking constantly. Add some grated nutmeg (if using). The cream is ready when it coats the whisk or a wooden spoon, about 10 minutes after all the milk is added.

Ingredient Tip: *Add 1/2 cup of grated Parmesan cheese to this sauce to enrich the flavor.*

BASIL PESTO
Pesto alla Genovese

PREP TIME: 10 MINUTES // **COOK TIME:** NONE // **YIELD:** 1 CUP

If there's one dish that captures the spirit of Liguria, it's basil pesto. A favorite no-cook sauce of this region (more specifically, from the city of Genoa), pesto's first mention dates back to the year 800. As with many sauce recipes, pesto varies in the exact amounts required to please, but here is a great start to get you going.

> 30 MINUTES OR LESS
> KID FRIENDLY
> FAMILY FRIENDLY
> VEGETARIAN

4 to 5 cups basil leaves

¼ teaspoon salt

1 or 2 garlic cloves

¼ cup extra-virgin olive oil, divided

¼ cup pine nuts

¼ cup grated Parmesan cheese, Pecorino cheese, or a combination of the two

1. Combine the basil, salt, and garlic in a food processor with about 2 tablespoons of oil. Pulse for several minutes, stopping occasionally to scrape the sides of the food processor.

2. Add the pine nuts and the remaining oil. Continue pulsing until a paste begins to form and the pine nuts are fully ground.

3. Add the cheese and pulse until a creamy paste is formed.

Prep Tip: A tablespoon of basil pesto adds fresh flavor to soups and other dishes, but prepping some on the fly is not always an option. Fortunately, pesto freezes wonderfully, so prepare a batch, spoon it into an ice cube tray, pop them out of the tray when frozen, and double-wrap them in plastic wrap and aluminum foil for use whenever needed.

SICILIAN PESTO
Pesto Siciliano

PREP TIME: 15 MINUTES // **COOK TIME:** NONE // **YIELD:** 1½ TO 2 CUPS

Perhaps not as famous as the basil pesto of Liguria, Sicilian pesto is no less tasty. Using ingredients that are famous in this region, such as tomatoes and ricotta cheese, this no-cook sauce can be added to pasta dishes or even used to top slices of toasted bread. Delicious and quick, this pesto is frequently prepared during the summer months, when it's too hot to cook elaborate dishes.

> 30 MINUTES OR LESS
> FAMILY FRIENDLY
> VEGETARIAN

1 pound tomatoes, halved
  and seeded
1 cup basil leaves
2 tablespoons pine nuts
½ cup grated Parmesan cheese
1 cup whole milk ricotta cheese
¼ cup extra-virgin olive oil
Salt

1. Combine the tomatoes, basil, pine nuts, Parmesan cheese, and ricotta in a food processor.

2. Pulse on low speed, stopping to check consistency, until thick and creamy.

3. In a slow stream, add the oil while quickly pulsing. Add more or less oil depending on your desired consistency. Additional oil will create a smoother pesto, whereas less oil will create a thicker one. Add salt to taste.

Substitution Tip: *Pine nuts can be expensive, but you can substitute almonds, walnuts, or pecans in this recipe and obtain similar results.*

BASIC WHITE RISOTTO
Risotto Bianco

PREP TIME: 10 MINUTES // **COOK TIME:** 20 MINUTES // **YIELD:** 4 SERVINGS

Although enjoyed throughout Italy, risotto is typically associated with the Lombardy region, where risotto, especially *risotto alla Milanese*, is a staple. Unlike many other Italian dishes that require little attention, risotto takes a bit more effort, as it needs constant stirring. The effort will reward you, however, with delightful taste and texture, so this is a dish worth mastering. To make this Milanese-style, add saffron and use beef stock.

> 30 MINUTES OR LESS
> KID FRIENDLY
> FAMILY FRIENDLY
> VEGETARIAN

6 cups **Quick Vegetable Broth** (page 39)

1 small onion, finely chopped

3 to 4 tablespoons olive oil

2 tablespoons butter

1 cup **arborio rice**

1 tablespoon finely chopped fresh parsley

½ cup grated **Parmesan cheese**

1. In a medium pan over low heat, heat the broth. Reduce the heat to very low, just to keep it warm.

2. In a large sauté pan over low heat, combine the onion, oil, and butter, and simmer.

3. Once the onion becomes translucent, add the rice and sauté for several minutes, stirring to coat the rice with the oil mixture. Add the parsley.

4. Add 1 cup of broth to the rice. Allow the rice to cook in the broth for 3 to 4 minutes or until the broth is fully absorbed by the rice. Continue the process of adding 1 cup of stock at a time until the rice is fully cooked, about 20 minutes.

5. Remove from the heat and add the cheese. Serve hot.

For Your Next Visit: Headed to Milan? Trattoria Da Abele on Via Temperanza offers a wide selection of risottos. Be sure to try a few during your stay.

RICE WITH PEAS
Risi e Bisi

PREP TIME: 5 MINUTES // **COOK TIME:** 25 MINUTES // **YIELD:** 4 TO 6 SERVINGS

A cross between risotto and a soup, *risi e bisi* is actually neither! A royal dish, frequently served to the Duke of Venice on April 25, the feast day of St. Mark, the patron saint of Venice, this dish has become a staple of Venetian cuisine. Although this dish is hundreds of years old, it is still very much served today, both in homes and at restaurants.

> 30 MINUTES OR LESS
> KID FRIENDLY
> FAMILY FRIENDLY

3 tablespoons olive oil

½ small onion, diced

¼ cup diced pancetta

1½ cups arborio rice

4 cups Quick Vegetable Broth (page 39), divided

Salt

12 ounces frozen peas

½ cup grated Parmesan cheese

1. In a large sauté pan over low heat, heat the oil. Add the onion and sauté for about 5 minutes. Add the pancetta and cook until the fat is rendered, about 2 minutes.

2. Add the rice and cook for about 1 minute, toasting the rice kernels. Add 2 cups of broth and continue cooking on medium-low heat for about 10 minutes. Add salt to taste.

3. Add the peas and remaining broth, and cook, stirring constantly, until the rice is creamy and tender, about 10 minutes more.

4. Remove the pan from the heat. Stir in the cheese and serve.

Ingredient Tip: *Want to make this dish vegetarian? Simply skip the pancetta.*

HOMEMADE PASTA
Pasta Fatta in Casa

PREP TIME: 15 MINUTES, PLUS INACTIVE TIME // **COOK TIME:** NONE // **YIELD:** 6 TO 8 SERVINGS

Enjoyed all over Italy, but particularly adored in Emilia-Romagna, fresh homemade pasta is everyone's favorite—and now you can make it, too! Whether it's for stuffed pasta such as ravioli, long shapes like fettuccini or spaghetti, or the foundation of homemade lasagna, fresh pasta is fun to prepare at home and a great family activity. It's also easier to prepare than you might expect. Compared to dry pasta, fresh pasta cooks in a fraction of the time, so adjust your cooking time accordingly. You don't need special tools—dough can be made by hand or machine.

> 30 MINUTES OR LESS
> KID FRIENDLY
> FAMILY FRIENDLY
> VEGETARIAN

1 cup semolina flour
1 cup all-purpose flour
3 large eggs, slightly beaten
1 tablespoon olive oil
1 tablespoon water
½ teaspoon salt

To make by hand

1. On a clean surface, combine the flours. Make a well in the middle, and add the rest of the ingredients. Knead by hand for at least 10 minutes until it bounces back when you poke it with your finger. If it doesn't bounce back it requires a few more minutes of kneading. If the dough is sticky, add an additional 1 to 2 tablespoons of semolina flour. If the dough is too stiff, add a few teaspoons of water, one teaspoon at a time. Allow the kneaded dough to rest for 30 minutes.

2. Divide the dough into quarters. Using a rolling pin, roll each piece to your desired thickness, ideally about ⅛-inch thick. Add some semolina flour to the surface if the dough is sticking.

3. Fresh pasta sheets can be cut into fettuccini or wide lasagna strips, or used with a ravioli press for stuffed pasta dishes.

To make by machine

1. Put all the ingredients in the mixing bowl of a stand mixer. Using the dough hook, mix for several minutes.

2. Test the dough for doneness as directed in step 1 above. Allow the dough to rest for 30 minutes.

3. Using a pasta machine, roll the dough to your desired thickness. Start with the widest setting on the machine. Using the dial knob on the machine, reduce the width until each sheet is about ⅛-inch thick.

4. Using the machine, fresh pasta sheets can be cut into fettuccini, linguini, or spaghetti by running the sheets through the cutting side of the machine.

Prep Tip: Fresh pasta can be refrigerated in a tightly closed resealable bag or airtight container for up to 2 days, or frozen for 2 to 3 weeks. Toss fresh pasta strands in a few tablespoons of flour before storing so they do not stick.

Substitution Tip: No semolina flour on hand? Fresh pasta can be made just by using all-purpose flour; it will be a bit less textured and less grainy, but no less delicious.

PASTA WITH BREAD CRUMBS
Fusilli alla Mollica

PREP TIME: 5 MINUTES // **COOK TIME:** 10 TO 12 MINUTES // **YIELD:** 4 TO 6 SERVINGS

Cucina povera or "poor man's cooking" is a traditional cooking style in southern Italy, and this recipe originates from Basilicata, located at the sole of Italy's boot. Today, the entire country has access to high-cost ingredients, but at one time, its residents made use of only a few inexpensive ingredients that were readily available. That said, making homemade bread crumbs with stale bread was a common practice, and that's how this recipe was born.

> 30 MINUTES OR LESS
> KID FRIENDLY
> FAMILY FRIENDLY

¾ pound **fusilli pasta** (or other pasta of choice)

3 tablespoons extra-virgin olive oil, plus more for drizzling

1 cup **fresh bread crumbs** (see tip)

5 or 6 **anchovies** (optional)

2 tablespoons chopped fresh parsley

½ cup grated **Pecorino Romano cheese** (or other grated cheese of choice)

1. Cook the pasta for 2 minutes less than instructed on the package. Drain, reserving ¼ cup of the pasta water.

2. Meanwhile, in a medium sauté pan over medium-high heat, heat the oil. Add the bread crumbs and toast for several minutes. Add the anchovies (if using), and cook with the crumbs until the anchovies break down and dissolve completely.

3. Add the pasta to the bread crumbs and toast for several additional minutes, mixing all the ingredients. If wetter pasta is desired, add a few tablespoons of the pasta water.

4. Add the parsley and cheese and remove from the heat. Top with an additional drizzle of oil. Serve immediately.

Ingredient Tip: When cooking with only a few ingredients, the quality of each is key. In this recipe, be sure to use bakery-style bread crumbs that are unflavored and unseasoned with additional ingredients.

LITTLE EARS WITH BROCCOLI RABE AND SAUSAGE
Orecchiette con Cime di Rapa e Salsiccia

PREP TIME: 10 MINUTES // **COOK TIME:** 20 MINUTES // **YIELD:** 4 SERVINGS

If you walk the streets of Puglia, you might see older housewives on their front lawns busy at work. Their delicate hands are expertly hand rolling a local specialty for which Puglia has become renowned. This specialty is fresh orecchiette pasta, which they will happily sell to tourists walking by. Puglia's preferred method of using orecchiette is to prepare it with broccoli rabe and sausages.

> 30 MINUTES OR LESS
> KID FRIENDLY
> FAMILY FRIENDLY

2 bunches broccoli rabe

Salt

12 ounces orecchiette pasta

4 tablespoons olive oil, plus more for drizzling

½ small onion, finely chopped

4 to 6 Italian sausages, casings removed

1. Trim the broccoli rabe by removing and discarding the lower ends and lower leaves, keeping just the florets. Bring a large pot of salted water to a boil. Boil the florets for 5 to 6 minutes. Using kitchen tongs, remove the florets from the boiling water and set aside.

2. Using the same water from the broccoli rabe, cook the orecchiette for 2 minutes less than directed on the package.

3. Meanwhile, in a large sauté pan over medium-high heat, heat the oil. Add the onion and sausages. Break the sausage up to resemble ground meat. Sauté for 7 to 8 minutes. Add the florets and stir to coat with the oil, cooking for an additional minute.

4. Drain the orecchiette, add them to the pan with the sausage, and cook for an additional 2 minutes. Serve hot and drizzle with more oil, if desired.

Substitution Tip: *If you cannot find broccoli rabe, you can substitute traditional broccoli. Simply use the tender florets and follow the same steps above.*

SPAGHETTI WITH CLAM SAUCE
Spaghetti con Vongole

PREP TIME: 10 MINUTES // **COOK TIME:** 15 MINUTES // **YIELD:** 4 SERVINGS

Located on the Adriatic coast of central Italy, Abbruzzo is in a wonderful strategic location to enjoy the cuisine of both land and sea. Lamb is the region's preferred meat of choice, and when it comes to shellfish, clams reign supreme. This dish takes just minutes to prepare and is a favorite of the region, thanks to its simplicity and old-school style of cooking. Much of Abbruzzo still remains undiscovered by tourism, and the simplicity of its people's lifestyle is evident in their cuisine.

> 30 MINUTES OR LESS

3 tablespoons olive oil, plus more for drizzling

1 garlic clove, minced

½ teaspoon salt

25 to 30 clams, scrubbed clean

½ cup dry white wine (see wine pairing tip)

12 ounces spaghetti

1 tablespoon chopped fresh parsley

1. In a large sauté pan over medium-high heat, heat the oil and garlic for about 1 minute. Add the salt, clams, and wine, cover, and cook for 5 minutes. Discard any unopened clams.

2. Meanwhile, cook the spaghetti in boiling salted water for 1 to 2 minutes less than directed on the package.

3. Drain the spaghetti and add to the pan with the clams. Finish cooking for an additional minute or two, or until the spaghetti is al dente. Transfer the pasta to a large serving bowl and sprinkle with the parsley. Top with an additional drizzle of oil, if desired.

Wine Pairing Tip: *Clams in wine sauce will go best with a dry sauvignon blanc. The same wine can be used in preparing the recipe.*

AMATRICIANA-STYLE BUCATINI
Bucatini all'Amatriciana

PREP TIME: 10 MINUTES // **COOK TIME:** 22 MINUTES // **YIELD:** 4 SERVINGS

Hailing from the town of Amatrice, this dish and its popularity extends far beyond Amatrice these days—in fact, it's become an Italian favorite. As with many Italian recipes, every home and restaurant has its own version, some using onions and wine as this recipe does, and some forgoing these ingredients.

> 30 MINUTES OR LESS
> FAMILY FRIENDLY

½ cup cubed **pancetta**

½ cup **dry white wine**

1 tablespoon olive oil

½ small onion, finely chopped

1 (28-ounce) can high-quality **crushed tomatoes** (see Choosing Quality Ingredients, page 5)

¾ pound **bucatini pasta** (or spaghetti)

Salt

½ cup grated **Pecorino Romano cheese**

1. In a sauté pan over medium heat, cook the pancetta for several minutes until the fat is rendered. With a slotted spoon, remove the pancetta from the pan, leaving the remaining fat in the pan.

2. To the pan, add the wine and cook, allowing the alcohol to evaporate. Add the oil and onion and cook for several minutes. Add the tomatoes and the pancetta, and cook the sauce for 15 to 18 minutes.

3. Meanwhile, cook the pasta in salted boiling water for 2 minutes less than directed on the package.

4. Drain the pasta and add it to the sauce, cooking for 2 additional minutes. Mix well to coat the pasta with the sauce.

5. Remove from the heat, stir in the cheese, and serve immediately.

Substitution Tip: *While Amatriciana sauce is traditionally made with guanciale, which is pork cheek, pancetta is often substituted, even in Italy. That said, if you cannot find either, thick bacon is a viable option.*

ANGRY PENNE
Penne Arrabbiata

PREP TIME: 5 MINUTES // **COOK TIME:** 20 MINUTES // **YIELD:** 4 TO 6 SERVINGS

A favorite of the city of Rome, as well as the region of Campania, *pasta arrabbiata* literally means "angry pasta." The "anger" refers to the spiciness in this sauce. As with any recipe using red pepper flakes, some trial and error will likely be necessary to achieve your ideal heat level. Test this recipe out a few times, using anywhere from ½ to 2 teaspoons of pepper flakes. You want good but palatable heat.

> 30 MINUTES OR LESS

3 tablespoons olive oil

½ to 2 teaspoons red pepper flakes

2 garlic cloves, minced

2 tablespoons chopped fresh parsley

3 cups canned diced tomatoes

1 pound penne or rigatoni pasta

Salt

Pecorino Romano cheese (optional)

1. In a large sauté pan over low heat, combine the oil and red pepper flakes and warm them for 1 to 2 minutes. Add the garlic and parsley, and cook for an additional minute.

2. Add the tomatoes and cook the sauce for an additional 15 to 18 minutes.

3. Meanwhile, cook the penne in salted boiling water for 2 minutes less than directed on the package. Drain the penne and add it to the sauce, mixing well so the pasta is coated. Cook together for 2 minutes.

4. Serve immediately, adding cheese if desired.

Substitution Tip: For a livelier dish, fresh vine-ripened tomatoes can be used instead of canned. Dice about 2 pounds of tomatoes and prepare the recipe as directed, adding a few minutes of cooking time to the sauce.

PASTA WITH CANNELLINI BEANS
Pasta e Fagioli

PREP TIME: 10 MINUTES // **COOK TIME:** 25 MINUTES // **YIELD:** 4 SERVINGS

It's common practice in the region of Friuli–Venezia Giulia to mix legumes with pasta. That said, this humble dish could be attributed to any region in Italy, as legumes are extremely popular and used by cooks around the entire country. Economical and healthy, beans are typically enjoyed in soups and pasta dishes in the fall and winter months, when the cold weather lends itself to heartier meals.

> 30 MINUTES OR LESS
> KID FRIENDLY
> FAMILY FRIENDLY
> VEGAN
> VEGETARIAN

1 small onion, chopped

2 garlic cloves, minced

2 tablespoons olive oil

1 teaspoon salt

2 cups canned crushed tomatoes

1 cup water

1½ cups elbow-shaped pasta

2 (16-ounce) cans cannellini beans, rinsed and drained

1. In a large sauté pan over low heat, combine the onion, garlic, oil, and salt, and simmer for 1 to 2 minutes, paying close attention that the garlic does not burn. Add the tomatoes and water, and simmer over low to medium heat for 18 minutes.

2. In the meantime, cook the pasta in salted boiling water as directed on the package.

3. When the sauce is cooked, add the beans. Over low heat, cook the beans and sauce for 5 minutes, gently folding the beans into the sauce.

4. Add the cooked pasta, and gently fold in all the ingredients to incorporate. Serve hot.

Substitution Tip: *Pasta e ceci, or pasta with chickpeas, can be prepared in the same way. You can also kick up the flavor by adding prosciutto, pancetta, or sausage to the sauce.*

NORCINA-STYLE PASTA
Pasta alla Norcina

PREP TIME: 10 MINUTES // **COOK TIME:** 25 MINUTES // **YIELD:** 4 SERVINGS

A classic dish from the city of Norcia in Umbria, this dish marries one of Umbria's key ingredients, sausages, with heavy cream. A local favorite in homes and restaurants, this dish, with its delicious white sauce, is sometimes combined with shaved black truffles.

> 30 MINUTES OR LESS
> FAMILY FRIENDLY

3 tablespoons olive oil

2 garlic cloves, minced

6 **pork sausages**, casings removed

½ cup **dry white wine**

¾ cup **heavy cream**

¾ pound **pasta**, such as rigatoni, ziti, or penne

Salt

¼ cup grated **Parmesan cheese**

1. In a large sauté pan over medium heat, combine the oil, garlic, and sausage. Use a wooden spoon to crumble the sausage until it resembles ground meat. Add the wine and cook for about 10 minutes.

2. Add the cream, reduce the heat to low, and cook for an additional 5 minutes. Meanwhile, cook the pasta in salted boiling water for 2 minutes less than directed on the package. Drain, reserving ¼ cup of the pasta water.

3. Add the pasta to the sauce, stirring well to coat the pasta. Continue cooking until the pasta is fully cooked and all the flavors are well incorporated. Add a few tablespoons of the pasta water if a thinner sauce is desired.

4. Remove from the heat and add the cheese, stirring well to incorporate. Serve immediately.

Substitution Tip: *While pork sausages are traditionally used in this dish, you can substitute chicken ones for a milder, tamer flavor.*

PASTA CARBONARA
Pasta alla Carbonara

PREP TIME: 10 MINUTES // **COOK TIME:** 15 MINUTES // **YIELD:** 4 TO 6 SERVINGS

One of the most recognizable Italian dishes, *spaghetti alla carbonara* has its origins in Rome, although now it's praised all over Italy and beyond. As with many recipes, specific origins are difficult to track down, but since the word *carbone* that carbonara is derived from means "charcoal," some believe it was a hearty dish created for serving to the *carbonari* (charcoal workers) after a hard day's work. The key to success with this dish: Make sure the eggs don't scramble.

> 30 MINUTES OR LESS
> KID FRIENDLY
> FAMILY FRIENDLY

12 ounces spaghetti

Salt

3 large eggs

¼ cup grated Pecorino Romano cheese, plus more for sprinkling

6 ounces diced pancetta (or 6 ounces thick-cut bacon, cubed)

3 tablespoons extra-virgin olive oil

1. Cook the spaghetti in salted boiling water for 2 minutes less than directed on the package.

2. In a small bowl, whisk the eggs and cheese. Mix well and set aside.

3. While the spaghetti is cooking, in a large sauté pan over medium heat, cook the pancetta until all the fat is rendered and it's crisp, 6 to 7 minutes.

4. When the pasta is almost cooked, add it to the oil and pancetta, tossing to combine. Reduce the heat to low, and add the egg and cheese mixture, stirring constantly to avoid scrambling the eggs. Cook for 1 minute, all the while stirring. Plate and top with additional cheese.

For Your Next Visit: *Headed to Rome? Be sure to try the spaghetti alla carbonara at Ristorante Pipero, on Corso Vittorio Emanuele.*

PASTA WITH GARLIC AND OLIVE OIL
Pasta Aglio e Olio

PREP TIME: 2 MINUTES // **COOK TIME:** 10 MINUTES // **YIELD:** 4 TO 6 SERVINGS

What do young adults cook after a night of dancing at the nightclubs? Why, *pasta aglio e olio*, of course! Once believed to be a peasant dish from Campania, this very humble recipe has now become a favorite to prepare post-dancing, due to its quickness and low-cost ingredients.

> 30 MINUTES OR LESS
> VEGETARIAN

16 ounces **spaghetti**
Salt
¼ cup extra-virgin olive oil
Red pepper flakes
4 large garlic cloves, minced
1 tablespoon chopped
  fresh parsley
¼ cup grated **Pecorino
  Romano cheese**

1. Cook the spaghetti in salted boiling water per the package instructions.

2. When the spaghetti is nearly cooked, in a medium sauté pan over low heat, heat the oil. Add red pepper flakes to taste and the garlic, and cook until the garlic turns color, paying close attention that it does not burn.

3. Drain the pasta, reserving some of the liquid. Add the spaghetti to the pan and toss well to coat. Add a few tablespoons of the pasta water and continue tossing until the water is evaporated.

4. Remove from the heat and add the parsley and cheese. Serve hot.

Substitution Tip: If you aren't a fan of red pepper flakes, leave them out. Instead, add a few salted anchovies. The anchovies will break down and melt away, providing a unique flavor that's very different than the pepper flakes.

PIZZA E PANE
Pizza and Bread

BASIC PIZZA DOUGH / *Impasto per la Pizza* **(Campania)** 68

MARGHERITA PIZZA / *Pizza Margherita* **(Campania)** 69

WHITE PIZZA / *Pizza Bianca* **(Campania)** 70

MARINARA PIZZA / *Pizza Marinara* **(Campania)** 71

BASIC FOCACCIA WITH BASIL / *Focaccia Genovese* **(Liguria)** 72

FOCACCIA WITH OLIVES AND PEPPER FLAKES /
Focaccia con Olive e Peperoncino **(Puglia)** 74

GRAPE FOCACCIA / *Schiacciata di Uva* **(Tuscany)** 76

FOCACCIA WITH PROSCIUTTO AND PARMESAN CHEESE /
Focaccia con Prosciutto e Parmigiano **(Emilia-Romagna)** 78

BASIC OLIVE BREAD / *Pane con Olive* **(Southern Italy)** 80

ITALIAN EASTER BREAD / *Cuzzupa Calabrese* **(Calabria)** 81

FRIED MINI PIZZAS / *Pizzette Fritte* **(Campania)** 83

More than a vessel for carrying toppings, pizza in Italy is an institution in itself. It is believed that the first pizza shop appeared in Naples in the eighteenth century. With its inexpensive ingredients, pizza was a humble treat reserved for the lower-middle class. Similar to pizza, but not quite the same, the origins of focaccia are a bit murkier, although the Ligurians like to take credit for it. Generally, red sauce is omitted in focaccias, and toppings are a bit scarcer. Bread baking at home is not unusual for Italians, especially in the cold winter months. Italy's love affair with carbs is evident with just one look at the dinner table.

BASIC PIZZA DOUGH
Impasto per la Pizza

PREP TIME: 20 MINUTES, PLUS INACTIVE TIME // **COOK TIME:** NONE // **YIELD:** 2 MEDIUM PIZZA CRUSTS

Although pizza hails from Naples, there isn't a region in Italy that doesn't love pizza. Knowing that pizza is a favorite of their school-age kids, Italian moms are used to making Saturday "pizza night." Now you can make any night an authentic pizza night. Perfecting the dough should be your first step; after that, the possibilities really are endless. See the prep tip if making by hand.

> 30 MINUTES OR LESS
> KID FRIENDLY
> FAMILY FRIENDLY
> VEGAN
> VEGETARIAN

¾ cup warm (not hot) water
2 teaspoons **rapid-rise yeast**
2½ cups all-purpose flour
1½ teaspoons salt
Olive oil, for greasing the bowl
  and pans

1. In the bowl of a stand mixer, combine the water and yeast, and mix well with a fork or whisk. Let stand for about 5 minutes.

2. Add the flour and salt and, using the dough hook attachment, mix for 6 to 9 minutes until a dough forms and it begins to pull from the sides of the bowl. Turn the dough out onto a floured surface and knead by hand for a few minutes, forming a ball.

3. Place the dough in an oiled bowl. Cover tightly with plastic wrap. Place in a draft-free location and allow time for the dough to double, from 1½ to 2 hours. Divide into 2 equal-size rounds and use immediately or freeze for future use.

Prep Tip: If mixing by hand, follow step 1 for the yeast. Place the flour and salt on a clean surface and create a well in the center. Add the yeast mixture, and mix the wet and dry ingredients. Knead by hand for 8 to 10 minutes until a smooth and elastic dough forms. Continue with step 3. While you're at it, consider doubling this recipe, using what you need and then freezing the rest of the dough. After thawing, allow the dough to stand at room temperature for 1 hour before stretching it into a pizza crust.

MARGHERITA PIZZA
Pizza Margherita

PREP TIME: 20 MINUTES, PLUS INACTIVE TIME // **COOK TIME:** 13 TO 18 MINUTES // **YIELD:** 2 MEDIUM PIZZAS

Margherita Pizza is probably the most famous pizza option in Italy and abroad, and how this name came to be is also very interesting. In 1889, Queen Margherita of Savoy visited Naples and asked the local *pizzaiolo* (pizza maker) to make her three pizzas so she could choose her favorite. Her preference was a simple tomato, basil, and mozzarella pizza, and henceforth, this was known as *Pizza Margherita*.

> 30 MINUTES OR LESS
> KID FRIENDLY
> FAMILY FRIENDLY
> VEGETARIAN

1 recipe Basic Pizza Dough
(page 68)
2 cups canned crushed
tomatoes
1 teaspoon dried oregano
Olive oil
2 cups shredded mozzarella
Basil leaves

1. Prepare the dough. Grease 2 (10-inch) round pizza pans or baking sheets, and roll or stretch the dough into shape. Preheat the oven to 500°F.

2. Top each pizza with 1 cup of tomatoes, sprinkle with the oregano, and top with a drizzle of oil. Divide the mozzarella between the two pizzas, sprinkling to evenly coat, leaving ½ inch of crust at the edge.

3. Bake the pizzas from 13 to 18 minutes, depending on your oven, until the crust is golden and the cheese is bubbly.

4. Transfer the pizzas to a large cutting board, top with fresh basil leaves, and allow to cool for a few minutes before cutting each into 8 slices.

For Your Next Visit: *Headed to Naples? Be sure to check out Sorbillo on Via dei Tribunali, in the city center. But pack your patience; regarded as having the best pizza in Naples, this restaurant can have a wait time as long as 2 hours.*

WHITE PIZZA
Pizza Bianca

PREP TIME: 20 MINUTES, PLUS INACTIVE TIME // **COOK TIME:** 13 TO 18 MINUTES // **YIELD:** 2 MEDIUM PIZZAS

In Italy, *Pizza Bianca* basically means any pizza without the tomato sauce. The toppings are only limited by your imagination, but they generally include hefty doses of cheeses, firm mozzarellas, anchovies, olives, sun-dried tomatoes, basil, and any other ingredient of choice, except of course, tomato sauce.

> 30 MINUTES OR LESS
> KID FRIENDLY
> FAMILY FRIENDLY

1 recipe Basic Pizza Dough
  (page 68)
1 tablespoon olive oil
8 ounces **provolone** slices, cut
  into strips
Salted anchovies (optional)
Dried oregano
Grated **Parmesan cheese**

1. Prepare the dough according to the recipe. Grease two (10-inch) round pizza pans or baking sheets, and roll or stretch the dough into shape. Score the pizza crust several times with a fork. Preheat the oven to 500°F.

2. Bake the pizza crusts for 10 minutes.

3. Remove the crusts from the oven and brush the tops with the olive oil. Evenly distribute the provolone slices on top. Add some salted anchovies (if using).

4. Sprinkle liberally with oregano and cheese. Place back in the oven and continue baking until the pizzas are golden and the crust is crisp, 3 to 8 minutes. Check the bottom for doneness.

Substitution Tip: *Like focaccia, pizza bianca can be used in place of bread. You can skip the provolone in the recipe and simply drizzle the dough with the oil and herbs. Prepare the pizza in a smaller pan for a thicker crust and use this as a flatbread. Flavored with herbs and grated Parmesan, this also makes great panini bread for prosciutto and Italian salami.*

MARINARA PIZZA
Pizza Marinara

PREP TIME: 20 MINUTES, PLUS INACTIVE TIME // **COOK TIME:** 13 TO 18 MINUTES // **YIELD:** 2 MEDIUM PIZZAS

Second in popularity only to the Margherita, and perhaps one of the simplest pizzas out there, is *Pizza Marinara*, which means "fisherman's pizza" or "pizza of the sea." However, unlike what the name implies, there is no seafood on this pizza. This pizza flavor, like many others, originated in the city of Naples, and it is called "marinara" because the basic ingredients have a long shelf life, making it ideal for fishermen to take along during their long voyages at sea.

> 30 MINUTES OR LESS
> KID FRIENDLY
> FAMILY FRIENDLY
> VEGAN
> VEGETARIAN

1 recipe Basic Pizza Dough
 (page 68)

3 cups canned crushed
 tomatoes

4 large garlic cloves,
 thinly sliced

2 teaspoons dried oregano

Olive oil

Freshly ground black pep-
 per (optional)

1. Prepare the dough according to the recipe. Grease two (10-inch) round pizza pans and roll or stretch the dough into shape. Preheat the oven to 500°F.

2. Working from the center out in a circular motion, spread about 1½ cups of tomatoes on top of each pizza, leaving a ½-inch border.

3. Top the pizzas with the garlic, oregano, and a drizzle of oil. Add some black pepper (if using).

4. Bake for 13 to 18 minutes or until the pizzas are golden and the crusts are crisp. Check the bottom for doneness.

Prep Tip: Due to the lack of toppings on this pizza, it lends itself well to freezing. Prepare the pizza as directed, cook halfway through, and remove from the oven. Cover well with aluminum foil before freezing. Thaw at room temperature before finishing the baking process.

BASIC FOCACCIA WITH BASIL
Focaccia Genovese

PREP TIME: 15 MINUTES, PLUS INACTIVE TIME // **COOK TIME:** 25 MINUTES // **YIELD:** 1 LARGE FOCACCIA

Focaccia is as popular in Italy as pizza, and every region has its own version. A cross between bread and pizza, focaccia typically goes lighter on the toppings. Used in place of bread next to salami and prosciutto, focaccia also makes a great antipasto with a glass of wine.

> 30 MINUTES OR LESS
> KID FRIENDLY
> FAMILY FRIENDLY
> VEGAN
> VEGETARIAN

1 packet **rapid-rise yeast**

1 teaspoon sugar

1½ cups warm water, divided

3 tablespoons olive oil, plus more for greasing, divided

5 to 6 cups all-purpose flour, divided

2 teaspoons salt

Extra-virgin olive oil, for drizzling

½ cup basil leaves, finely chopped

1. In the mixing bowl of a stand mixer, combine the yeast, sugar, and ½ cup of warm water. Let stand for several minutes.

2. Add the remaining 1 cup of warm water, 3 tablespoons of oil, 5 cups of flour, and the salt. Using the dough hook attachment, mix the dough on low speed for 5 to 6 minutes. If the dough is sticky, add more flour as needed, up to 1 additional cup.

3. Transfer the dough to a large oiled bowl. Cover with plastic wrap and allow to double in size, 1 to 2 hours.

4. Punch the dough down and generously oil a baking sheet. Add the dough to the baking sheet and spread it to the edge of the pan. Loosely cover and allow 30 to 40 minutes for a second rise. Preheat the oven to 400°F.

5. Indent the dough all over the top with your thumbs, drizzle with oil, and bake for 20 minutes. Remove from the oven, drizzle with extra-virgin olive oil, and sprinkle with the basil. Bake for an additional 5 to 7 minutes.

Prep Tip: *If preparing by hand, follow step 1. Place 5 cups of flour on a clean surface and create a well in the center. Add 1 more cup of warm water, the oil, and the yeast mixture in the center, and using a fork or your fingertips, bring the flour inward toward the center until the flour absorbs all the liquid. Add up to 1 cup of additional flour, if needed. Knead the dough by hand for 7 to 8 minutes and continue with the remaining steps.*

For Your Next Visit: *Be sure to swing by Focacceria Genovese on Piazza Fossatello on your next visit to Genoa for some delicious basil focaccia.*

FOCACCIA WITH OLIVES AND PEPPER FLAKES
Focaccia con Olive e Peperoncino

PREP TIME: 15 MINUTES, PLUS INACTIVE TIME // **COOK TIME:** 25 TO 30 MINUTES // **YIELD:** 1 LARGE FOCACCIA

The town of Bari, in Puglia, is renowned for its focaccias. Frequently topped with cherry tomatoes or black olives, focaccias are served as a snack between meals, as an antipasto, or in place of bread during a meal. Bake shops prepare focaccia throughout the day to satisfy that craving at any given time. Focaccia can be appreciated and enjoyed any time of day.

> 30 MINUTES OR LESS
> VEGAN
> VEGETARIAN

1 packet **rapid-rise yeast**

1 teaspoon sugar

1½ cups warm water, divided

3 tablespoons olive oil, plus more for greasing

5 to 6 cups all-purpose flour

2 teaspoons salt

¾ cup **pitted black olives**

Red pepper flakes

1 teaspoon dried oregano

Sea salt

1. In the mixing bowl of a stand mixer, combine the yeast, sugar, and ½ cup of warm water. Let stand for several minutes.

2. Add the remaining 1 cup of warm water, the oil, 5 cups of flour, and the salt. Using the dough hook attachment, mix the dough on low speed for 5 to 6 minutes. If the dough is very moist, add some additional flour, up to 1 more cup.

3. Transfer the dough to a large oiled bowl. Allow it to double in size, 1 to 2 hours.

4. Punch the dough down and generously oil a baking sheet. Place the dough on the baking sheet and spread it to the edge of the pan. Indent all over the top with your thumbs.

5. Add the pitted olives, red pepper flakes, and oregano on top of the focaccia. Sprinkle sea salt on top. Allow to rise for about another 30 minutes.

6. Bake 25 to 30 minutes until crispy and golden.

Prep Tip: Like pizza dough, focaccia dough freezes very well, so make some dough in advance and store it in the freezer. Thaw the dough overnight in the refrigerator or on the counter, then place it on a baking sheet (as in step 4) and leave it out on the sheet for 20 minutes to rise before baking.

GRAPE FOCACCIA
Schiacciata di Uva

PREP TIME: 20 MINUTES, PLUS INACTIVE TIME // **COOK TIME:** 15 TO 20 MINUTES // **YIELD:** 1 LARGE FOCACCIA

The term *schiacciata* literally means "flatten down" in Italian, and it can refer to anything from breads to pressed sandwiches or panini. In September, during grape harvest time in Tuscany, home bakers prep this sweet and savory treat as a way to use the seasonal crop of grapes. It's also found in bakeries and bread shops throughout Tuscany. The grapes burst with flavor when baked, making this a delicious treat to enjoy with a nice glass of wine.

> 30 MINUTES OR LESS
> KID FRIENDLY
> FAMILY FRIENDLY
> VEGETARIAN

1 packet **rapid-rise yeast**

1 teaspoon sugar

1½ cups warm water, divided

3 tablespoons olive oil, plus more for greasing

5 to 6 cups all-purpose flour, plus extra

2 teaspoons salt

3 tablespoons butter, melted

1 pound **Concord grapes**

3 to 5 tablespoons coarse raw sugar

1. In the mixing bowl of a stand mixer, combine the yeast, sugar, and ½ cup of warm water. Let stand for several minutes.

2. Add the remaining 1 cup of warm water, the oil, 5 cups of flour, and the salt. Using the dough hook attachment, mix the dough on low speed for 5 to 6 minutes. If the dough is very moist, add some additional flour, up to 1 more cup.

3. Transfer the dough to a large oiled bowl. Allow to double in size, 1 to 2 hours.

4. Preheat the oven to 400°F.

5. Generously grease a baking sheet, place the dough on it, and stretch the dough out to the sides. Use your thumbs to indent the focaccia. Brush the focaccia with the melted butter.

6. Press the grapes into the dough and sprinkle with the raw sugar. Bake 25 to 30 minutes until the focaccia is crispy and golden.

Substitution Tip: *This delicious recipe yields a sweet treat after a meal. However, it's very easy to turn this into a savory treat instead. Use oil in place of butter, and add some sea salt in place of the raw sugar. You can also top this with some rosemary for a hint of herb flavor.*

FOCACCIA WITH PROSCIUTTO AND PARMESAN CHEESE
Focaccia con Prosciutto e Parmigiano

PREP TIME: 15 MINUTES, PLUS INACTIVE TIME // **COOK TIME:** 25 MINUTES // **YIELD:** 1 LARGE FOCACCIA

Two key ingredients are prominent in Emilia-Romagna: Parmigiano cheese and prosciutto ham. Both from the area of Parma, these two ingredients are found in many dishes throughout Italy, but particularly in this region. Eaten as antipasti on their own, in sandwiches at school or work, or perhaps added to baked pastas and lasagnas, these two ingredients find their way into just about every course. They also make wonderful toppings on pizzas and focaccias. This is just one example.

> 30 MINUTES OR LESS
> KID FRIENDLY
> FAMILY FRIENDLY

1 packet **rapid-rise yeast**

1 teaspoon sugar

1½ cups warm water, divided

3 tablespoons olive oil, plus more for greasing

5 to 6 cups all-purpose flour, plus extra

2 teaspoons salt

Extra-virgin olive oil, for drizzling

½ cup shaved **Parmesan cheese**

¼ pound sliced **prosciutto**, torn into bits

Rosemary leaves

Sea salt

1. In the mixing bowl of a stand mixer, combine the yeast, sugar, and ½ cup of warm water. Let stand for several minutes.

2. Add the remaining 1 cup of warm water, the oil, 5 cups of flour, and the salt. Using the dough hook attachment, mix the dough on low speed for 5 to 6 minutes. If the dough is very moist, add some additional flour, up to 1 more cup.

3. Transfer the dough to a large oiled bowl. Allow it to double in size, 1 to 2 hours.

4. Generously oil a baking sheet, place the dough on it, and stretch the dough out to the sides. Use your thumbs to indent the focaccia all over. Drizzle generously with several tablespoons of extra-virgin olive oil.

5. Bake the plain focaccia for 20 minutes until just slightly golden brown.

6. Remove the focaccia from the oven and top with the cheese, prosciutto, and rosemary leaves. Carefully add salt to taste, as both Parmesan and prosciutto add salt. Bake for an additional 7 to 8 minutes until the focaccia is golden brown and crisp at the corners.

For Your Next Visit: As a leader of culinary tours to Italy, one of my favorite regions is Emilia-Romagna. For a real treat, be sure to visit an authentic Parmigiano cheese factory to see how the indisputable king of cheese is made.

BASIC OLIVE BREAD
Pane con Olive

PREP TIME: 20 MINUTES, PLUS INACTIVE TIME // **COOK TIME:** 35 MINUTES // **YIELD:** 1 ROUND LOAF

Driving around southern Italy, you will encounter endless miles of olive trees growing under the fierce summer sun. The south makes use of these fruits by pressing them into olive oil, curing them with oil and salt, and adding them to countless dishes such as breads, antipasti, or pizza. For this bread, be sure to use olives that are flavorful and pungent.

> 30 MINUTES OR LESS
> FAMILY FRIENDLY
> VEGAN
> VEGETARIAN

2 teaspoons **rapid-rise yeast**

2¾ to 3 cups all-purpose flour

1 cup lukewarm water

½ teaspoon salt

2 teaspoons olive oil, plus more for greasing

¾ cup **olives** of your choice, pitted and halved

1. In the bowl of a stand mixer, combine the yeast, 2¾ cups of flour, the water, salt, and olive oil. Gently mix the ingredients using the dough hook attachment until the dough begins to form. Let stand for 10 to 15 minutes.

2. Add the olives and knead for 5 minutes on medium speed. If the dough is sticky, slowly add the remaining ¼ cup of flour. Transfer the dough to a clean surface and knead by hand for a few minutes.

3. Place the dough in an oiled bowl. Allow it to rise in a draft-free location for 1 to 1½ hours, to double in size.

4. Punch the dough down and shape it into a round loaf. Place it on a baking sheet lined with parchment paper. Loosely cover with plastic wrap and let stand to allow to double in size again, 45 minutes to 1 hour.

5. Meanwhile, preheat the oven to 400°F. Bake for 30 to 35 minutes.

Substitution Tip: Sun-dried tomatoes make an excellent substitution in this recipe for the olives, or try a combination of the two.

ITALIAN EASTER BREAD
Cuzzupa Calabrese

PREP TIME: 20 MINUTES, PLUS INACTIVE TIME // **COOK TIME:** 40 MINUTES // **YIELD:** 1 LARGE BREAD

Served during Easter time, *cuzzupa Calabrase,* as it is known in dialect, is bread that is prepared out of sweet, buttery dough. Frequently served at breakfast and topped with jam, this bread is often prepared by placing three uncooked eggs, still in their shells, on top of the dough, and then it's baked. The eggs are mostly for show, as they are generally tossed afterward.

> 30 MINUTES OR LESS
> KID FRIENDLY
> FAMILY FRIENDLY
> VEGETARIAN

1¼ cups whole milk

2¼ teaspoons rapid-rise yeast

Pinch salt

5½ tablespoons butter, softened

2 eggs, beaten

½ cup sugar

3½ cups all-purpose flour, plus up to 1 cup more, if needed

Olive oil, for greasing

1. In a small saucepan over medium-high heat, heat the milk until small bubbles form at the edge. Remove from the heat and transfer the milk into a bowl to cool until lukewarm.

2. In the bowl of a stand mixer, combine the yeast, milk, salt, butter, eggs, and sugar. Using the dough hook attachment, mix until just combined. Add about half the flour and mix until smooth.

3. Slowly add the rest of the flour until a stiff dough forms. Add additional flour, if needed, until the dough is no longer sticky. Knead until smooth.

4. Place the dough in a greased bowl. Cover and let rise in a warm place until the dough has doubled, 45 minutes to 1 hour.

5. Punch the dough down and divide it into three equal pieces. Roll each piece to form a thick rope about 12 inches long. Starting from the top, form a braid.

Continued

6. Place the braid on a baking sheet lined with parchment paper.

7. Cover with plastic wrap or a clean kitchen towel and let the dough rise a second time, until doubled, 45 minutes to 1 hour.

8. Preheat the oven to 350°F and bake until golden, about 40 minutes. Cool on a rack.

Substitution Tip: To add even more flavor to this bread, feel free to add lemon or orange zest, or both.

FRIED MINI PIZZAS
Pizzette Fritte

PREP TIME: 10 MINUTES, PLUS INACTIVE TIME // **COOK TIME:** 5 MINUTES // **YIELD:** 15 TO 20 SMALL PIZZAS

As if pizza wasn't delicious enough as is, here's a new way that many home cooks in Italy are using leftover pizza dough. Fried pizzas, or *pizzette fritte*, are also known as *zeppole*, and they are topped with items such as herbs, cheeses, and anchovies—even powdered sugar or jams. They make a great antipasto or snack between meals.

> 30 MINUTES OR LESS
> KID FRIENDLY
> FAMILY FRIENDLY
> VEGETARIAN

2 cups all-purpose flour
1 teaspoon salt
1 tablespoon olive oil
1 teaspoon **rapid-rise yeast**
¼ to ¾ cup warm water
Olive oil, for greasing
Vegetable oil, for frying
Rosemary leaves
Sea salt
Grated **Parmesan cheese**

1. On a clean surface, create a mound with the flour. Add the salt, olive oil, and yeast, and mix. Slowly add some warm water, anywhere from ¼ to ¾ cup, until a soft, elastic dough is formed. Knead for several minutes.

2. Place the dough in an oiled bowl, cover, and allow to rise until doubled in size, 1½ to 2 hours.

3. When doubled, pull small balls of dough, and use a rolling pin or your hands to shape the dough into very small pizzas. It's perfectly acceptable (in fact, desired) for the pizzas to have an odd shape and not be perfectly round.

4. Heat the vegetable oil to 350°F. Plunge the pizzette in the hot oil, and brown them on both sides for several minutes. Remove from the oil, place on paper towels, and top with rosemary leaves, sea salt, and cheese.

Substitution Tip: *Make these small pizzette into something sweet by skipping the rosemary, sea salt, and cheese, and smearing them with a bit of butter and some cinnamon sugar instead.*

CARNE
Meat

BEEF RAGÙ / *Ragù Semplice di Manzo* **(Southern Italy)** 86

EASY BEEF BRACIOLE / *Braciole di Manzo Facilissima* **(Southern Italy)** 87

BEEF IN PIZZA-STYLE SAUCE / *Carne alla Pizzaiola* **(Campania)** 88

BEEF SOUP / *Bollito di Carne di Manzo* **(Tuscany)** 89

BALSAMIC VINEGAR STEAK / *Filetto al Aceto Balsamico* **(Emilia-Romagna)** 91

PORK WITH OLIVES / *Maiale con Olive* **(Sicily)** 92

OVEN-BAKED PORK CHOPS / *Cotolette di Maiale al Forno* **(Emilia-Romagna)** 93

MOLISE-STYLE PORK WITH PEPPERS / *Maiale Molisano con Peperoni* **(Molise)** 94

ROASTED SAUSAGES WITH POTATOES AND BELL PEPPERS / *Salsiccie al Forno con Patate e Peperoni* **(Calabria)** 95

SAUSAGE WITH MUSHROOMS AND TOMATOES / *Salsiccia con Funghi e Pomodori* **(Piedmont)** 96

MILAN-STYLE PORK CHOPS / *Cotolette alla Milanese* **(Lombardy)** 97

While the Mediterranean diet is highly praised for its emphasis on legumes, grains, fruits, and vegetables, Italians also appreciate and eat meat. Traditionally offered as a second course or eaten at dinner, whereas pastas and rice are eaten at lunch, meat in Italy is served on a regular basis, although the portions aren't as large as they are in the United States. Chicken, while plentiful in the countryside of Italy, is eaten less frequently than pork, veal, or beef. The recipes in this chapter are quick enough to prep on a weeknight, but also guest worthy for a Saturday night dinner party.

BEEF RAGÙ
Ragù Semplice di Manzo

PREP TIME: 5 MINUTES // **COOK TIME:** 35 MINUTES // **YIELD:** 4 TO 6 SERVINGS

Ragù sauce in Italy is a Sunday tradition. Consisting of a variety of meats, sausages, and perhaps even meatballs, ragù really can contain whatever meat you like, as there are no rules for what one should put in it. Frequently, the sauce is used as a condiment to a first course of pasta, or one can opt to just enjoy the meat. I prefer using some very tender steak tips, as they cook quickly, are flavorful, and can be found at any grocery store.

> 30 MINUTES OR LESS
> FAMILY FRIENDLY
> GLUTEN FREE
> DAIRY FREE

3 tablespoons olive oil

½ small onion, chopped

1 tablespoon chopped
   fresh parsley

1 tablespoon chopped
   fresh basil

1½ to 2 pounds steak tips

1 teaspoon salt

1 garlic clove, minced

1 (28-ounce) can crushed
   tomatoes

1 cup water

1. In a large saucepan over medium heat, heat the oil and sauté the onion, parsley, and basil.

2. Add the steak tips and brown on all sides, turning several times to ensure the meat is not burning. Add the salt.

3. Stir in the garlic and tomatoes. Add the water, stir, reduce the heat to low, and simmer for 30 minutes.

Prep Tip: Many Italians make their Sunday ragù the day before, as the flavors intensify overnight. So, if you are having guests, don't feel guilty about getting a head start and prepping this sauce in advance—just be sure to heat it up fully before serving.

EASY BEEF BRACIOLE
Braciole di Manzo Facilissima

PREP TIME: 10 MINUTES // **COOK TIME:** 25 MINUTES // **YIELD:** 4 SERVINGS

Braciole consists of any meat, chicken, fish, or even vegetable that is thinly sliced and stuffed in some fashion, then rolled up and cooked, generally in red sauce. In southern Italy, braciole is often made with a thin slice of beef or veal stuffed with some ham, salami, cheeses, and even slices of hard-boiled eggs, with a bit of grated Parmesan added. A combination of these ingredients makes for a delectable stuffing.

> FAMILY FRIENDLY

½ onion, chopped

2 tablespoons olive oil

1 (28-ounce) can crushed tomatoes

8 thin slices beef rump or bottom round

Salt

Freshly ground black pepper

8 thin slices deli-style salami or prosciutto

8 thin slices provolone cheese

Parsley sprigs, stemmed

½ cup grated Parmesan cheese

1. In a large sauté pan, sauté the onion in the oil for a few minutes. Add the tomatoes and simmer.

2. In the meantime, prepare the braciole by sprinkling the meat slices with salt and pepper.

3. Place a slice of salami or prosciutto and cheese on top of each slice of meat. Add a few sprigs of parsley, and sprinkle some Parmesan cheese on top.

4. Roll up the meat tightly and, using a long toothpick, secure the meat closed. Repeat with the remaining meat.

5. Add the 8 braciole to the simmering sauce and cook for 25 minutes. Be sure to remove the toothpick before plating and serving.

Wine Pairing: *Red meat goes wonderfully with a bold red wine, so enjoy a nice Chianti with these tender beef braciole.*

BEEF IN PIZZA-STYLE SAUCE
Carne alla Pizzaiola

PREP TIME: 5 MINUTES // **COOK TIME:** 15 MINUTES // **YIELD:** 4 SERVINGS

Using primarily the same ingredients as the Pizza Marinara (page 71), the sauce for this quick second course consists of just tomatoes, garlic, and oregano. These few basic ingredients transform into a delicious sauce that can be used to dress a few ounces of pasta or simply get mopped up with some crusty bread. The exact recipe varies from house to house, but the key ingredients remain the same.

> 30 MINUTES OR LESS
> KID FRIENDLY
> FAMILY FRIENDLY
> GLUTEN FREE

2 tablespoons olive oil

1 garlic clove, cut in half

2½ cups canned
 crushed tomatoes

½ cup cold water

Salt

Freshly ground black pepper

1 pound thin beef slices

1 teaspoon dried oregano

1. In a sauté pan over low heat, heat the oil. Add the garlic and cook for 1 minute. Add the tomatoes, water, and salt and pepper to taste, and simmer for 10 minutes.

2. Sprinkle the beef slices with salt and pepper. Add the beef to the pan, and use a spoon to cover them with the sauce. Add the dried oregano.

3. Cover the pan and simmer until the meat is fully cooked, 4 to 5 minutes, turning once halfway through.

4. Plate a few pieces of meat, top with some sauce, and serve immediately.

Substitution Tip: While delicious just as prepared here, you can kick this dish up a bit by adding black olives or capers.

BEEF SOUP
Bollito di Carne di Manzo

PREP TIME: 10 MINUTES // **COOK TIME:** 40 TO 60 MINUTES // **YIELD:** 4 SERVINGS

Tuscans and northern Italians eat a good amount of beef, and this soup is just one way of using the tougher cuts. This makes a delicious light meal in itself, or you can add a bit of small cut pasta to the broth to make it more substantial. This is typically a wintry soup, and with added pasta, it can be served as a first course, or the meat can be separated and eaten as a second course.

> FAMILY FRIENDLY

> GLUTEN FREE

> DAIRY FREE

2 teaspoons salt, or more

3 carrots, peeled and diced into 2-inch pieces

2 celery stalks, cut into 5 to 7 pieces

1 large onion, quartered

Small handful parsley sprigs, stemmed

1 cup diced fresh or canned tomatoes

2 pounds various cuts of beef

1. Put all the ingredients in a large soup pot. Add enough water to fill the pot to a few inches below the top.

2. Boil the soup for 40 minutes to 1 hour, depending on the cuts of beef used. Tender cuts will take closer to 40 minutes, while tougher cuts will take closer to 1 hour. Skim off any beef fat that rises to the top.

3. Serve this soup as a first course. You can also strain and discard all the non-meat ingredients, chop up the meat, and serve just the broth and the meat.

Substitution Tip: If you are not into beef, use the same exact recipe to make chicken soup. Any cut of chicken will do. Bone-in pieces will give you a fattier broth than boneless and skinless cuts.

BALSAMIC VINEGAR STEAK
Filetto al Aceto Balsamico

PREP TIME: 5 MINUTES // **COOK TIME:** 8 MINUTES // **YIELD:** 4 SERVINGS

Traditional balsamic vinegar of Modena is a highly praised and expensive condiment made only in Emilia-Romagna. Made from grape must (the by-product of the pressed grapes) and aged at least 12 years, this specific ingredient is regulated by the Italian government. Most recipes use regular balsamic vinegar of Modena, which is a variety of balsamic vinegar that is much cheaper and with far less stringent regulations (see Choosing Quality Ingredients, page 5).

> 30 MINUTES OR LESS
> FAMILY FRIENDLY
> DAIRY FREE

½ cup balsamic vinegar

¼ cup olive oil, plus 1 tablespoon, divided

1 teaspoon chopped fresh parsley

2 garlic cloves, minced

4 (5-ounce) boneless rib eye steaks, such as Delmonico

Salt

Freshly ground black pepper

1. In a small bowl, mix the balsamic vinegar, ¼ cup of oil, parsley, and garlic. Brush the steaks with the marinade, and season with salt and pepper.

2. In a large skillet over medium heat, heat the remaining 1 tablespoon of olive oil. When the oil is hot, add the steaks to the pan, reserving the remaining marinade. Cook the steaks to your desired doneness, 3 to 4 minutes per side for medium-rare.

3. Once cooked, remove the steaks from the pan and place them on a plate, covering them with aluminum foil.

4. Add the leftover marinade to the hot pan, cook for 2 to 3 minutes until the marinade is reduced by half. Uncover the steaks and pour the reduced glaze on top.

Substitution Tip: While traditionally prepared with beef, this same marinade can be used for thin chicken breasts.

PORK WITH OLIVES
Maiale con Olive

PREP TIME: 10 MINUTES // **COOK TIME:** 25 MINUTES // **YIELD:** 4 SERVINGS

Pork dishes are prominent in southern Italy, as are olives, so it's no surprise that this dish combining both has its origins in Sicily. Tender, economical, and very flavorful, this dish makes an ideal second course for a quick weeknight dinner, but it's also sophisticated enough to serve guests at a get-together. Cut the pork tenderloin pieces into whatever size you prefer; the smaller the pieces, the faster they will cook.

> 30 MINUTES OR LESS
> FAMILY FRIENDLY
> DAIRY FREE

1 small **pork tenderloin**, cut into 1½-inch-thick rounds

½ cup flour

Salt

Freshly ground black pepper

¼ cup olive oil

3 sprigs **rosemary**, leaves only, stemmed

1 cup **dry white wine**

½ cup **green olives**, pitted and halved

1. Gently coat the pork tenderloin pieces in the flour. Season with salt and pepper. Set aside.

2. In a large sauté pan over medium-high heat, heat the oil and rosemary for a few minutes.

3. Add the pork to the oil and brown on all sides. Add the white wine and olives.

4. Reduce the heat to low, and continue cooking the pork for an additional 15 to 20 minutes, uncovered. If the juices are drying up too quickly, reduce the heat and add a little bit of water. A little bit of juice should remain to top the meat with before serving.

Substitution Tip: *While pork is the preferred meat of southern Italy, this same exact recipe is delicious using boneless and skinless chicken thighs. Add additional aromatics such as parsley, basil, sage, or bay leaves for added flavor.*

OVEN-BAKED PORK CHOPS
Cotolette di Maiale al Forno

PREP TIME: 10 MINUTES // **COOK TIME:** 20 TO 25 MINUTES // **YIELD:** 4 SERVINGS

Frequently served with a simple green salad and a wedge of lemon for squeezing on top, these pork chops come together quickly, and then the oven does the rest of the work. Their flavorful outer coating combines bread crumbs with the indisputable king of cheeses from Emilia-Romagna—authentic Parmesan cheese.

> 30 MINUTES OR LESS
> KID FRIENDLY
> FAMILY FRIENDLY

Nonstick cooking spray

1 cup **bread crumbs**

½ cup grated **Parmesan cheese**

4 **bone-in pork chops**

Salt

Freshly ground black pepper

2 **eggs**, lightly beaten

Olive oil, for drizzling

1. Preheat the oven to 375°F. Spray a baking sheet with cooking spray and set aside.

2. In a medium bowl, stir together the bread crumbs and cheese.

3. Sprinkle the pork chops with salt and pepper, and dip them in the beaten eggs. Coat the chops in the bread crumb and cheese mixture and gently place them on the prepared baking sheet. Add a light drizzle of oil.

4. Bake for 20 to 25 minutes, depending on the thickness of the chops. Gently, so as not to remove any of the outer coating, turn the chops over once midway through baking.

Substitution Tip: Instead of baking these, you can fry them in vegetable oil. Simply add several inches of oil to a large frying pan, heat the oil, and fry them until crisp and golden.

MOLISE-STYLE PORK WITH PEPPERS
Maiale Molisano con Peperoni

PREP TIME: 5 MINUTES // **COOK TIME:** 15 MINUTES // **YIELD:** 4 SERVINGS

Molise is one of the smallest regions in southern Italy. It was once under the rule of Sicily, and the Sicilian influence is still evident in their cuisine. Dishes with olives, capers, tomatoes, and lots of olive oil are plentiful. Pork and lamb are the preferred meats of Molise, and for this dish, you can easily substitute one for the other.

> 30 MINUTES OR LESS
> FAMILY FRIENDLY
> GLUTEN FREE
> DAIRY FREE

1 **bell pepper** (red, green, or yellow), seeded and cut into thin strips

1 pound **cherry tomatoes**, halved

4 tablespoons olive oil, divided

Salt

Freshly ground black pepper

4 **bone-in pork chops**, about 1 inch thick

½ cup **black olives**, pitted

1. Preheat the broiler portion of the oven.

2. Toss the pepper strips and cherry tomatoes together with 3 tablespoons of oil. Add salt and pepper to taste. Spread the vegetables in a single layer on a baking pan.

3. Brush the chops with the remaining 1 tablespoon of oil, sprinkle with salt and pepper, and place the chops on top of the vegetables.

4. Bake the chops under the broiler for 6 to 7 minutes. Turn the chops over, scatter the olives on top, and cook for an additional 6 to 7 minutes until fully cooked. Serve the chops, spooning the vegetables and juices on top.

Substitution Tip: In Molise, this dish is usually prepared with pork, but you can also swap out the pork for boneless chicken thighs or tenders.

ROASTED SAUSAGES WITH POTATOES AND BELL PEPPERS
Salsiccie al Forno con Patate e Peperoni

PREP TIME: 10 MINUTES // **COOK TIME:** 35 TO 40 MINUTES // **YIELD:** 4 TO 6 SERVINGS

Sausages, potatoes, and peppers: These are ingredients that, while readily available all over Italy, are very prominent in Calabria. This homey dish is eaten mostly during winter months, when pork products are cured and sausages are at their freshest. In Calabria, it's not uncommon to cook this dish by the open fire in a terra cotta pan. The smell of roasted peppers engulfs the entire house and remains present even a day or two afterward.

> 30 MINUTES OR LESS
> FAMILY FRIENDLY
> GLUTEN FREE
> DAIRY FREE

4 **bell peppers** (red, green, orange, or a combination), seeded and cut into strips

6 **hot pork sausages**, cut into 4 pieces

4 or 5 medium **potatoes**, peeled and cubed

¼ cup olive oil, plus extra for greasing

Rosemary leaves

1 large onion, sliced

Salt

Freshly ground black pepper

1. Preheat the oven to 400°F. Place an empty large roasting pan or rimmed baking sheet in the oven to heat.

2. In a large bowl, combine the peppers, sausages, potatoes, oil, rosemary, and onion. Using clean hands or a spatula, mix all the ingredients well. Season with salt and pepper.

3. Add a few tablespoons of oil to the heated pan, and add all the ingredients, spreading evenly. Bake for 35 to 40 minutes. Using a wooden spoon or spatula, turn the ingredients once or twice while roasting to ensure they are not sticking to the pan.

Substitution Tip: Mushrooms, olives, and fresh tomatoes make great additions or substitutions in this recipe. Add additional Italian herbs as desired.

SAUSAGE WITH MUSHROOMS AND TOMATOES
Salsiccia con Funghi e Pomodori

PREP TIME: 10 MINUTES // **COOK TIME:** 25 MINUTES // **YIELD:** 4 SERVINGS

Piedmont is praised for its mushrooms, and this is just one way residents prepare them. In Piedmont, mushrooms find their way into first courses, such as soups and stews, and are often combined with sausages or other meats. Delicious paired with local wine, this dish is frequently served at home as well as at many of the local restaurants or *trattorie*.

> 30 MINUTES OR LESS
> GLUTEN-FREE
> DAIRY FREE

1 pound sweet or hot Italian sausages

1½ cups red wine, divided

1 cup water

3 tablespoons olive oil

2 garlic cloves, sliced

Pinch salt

1 cup canned crushed tomatoes

2 pounds white button or cremini mushrooms, or a combination, cleaned and quartered

1. With a toothpick or fork, score the sausages at least a dozen times. Put them in a small soup pot, cover with 1 cup of red wine and the water, and boil for 15 minutes.

2. In a medium sauté pan over low heat, cook the oil, garlic, and salt for 1 minute. Add the tomatoes and cook for 5 minutes.

3. Add the mushrooms and the remaining ½ cup of wine. Meanwhile, drain the sausages, rinse them under cold water, and cut them into 4 or 5 pieces each.

4. Add them to the sauce and cook an additional 7 to 8 minutes until fully cooked and all the ingredients have been well incorporated.

Wine Pairing: *While the initial wine used to boil the sausages is discarded, the flavor is infused in the sausages, so opt for an inexpensive-but-worthy red to go with this dish.*

MILAN-STYLE PORK CHOPS
Cotolette alla Milanese

PREP TIME: 10 MINUTES // **COOK TIME:** 25 MINUTES // **YIELD:** 4 SERVINGS

A specialty of the city of Milan, this is prepared in homes as well as served at countless restaurants across the city. This dish is typically made with a veal cutlet, known for its buttery flavor, and is crispy on the outside and soft on the inside. Because veal is not as readily available in the United States, this recipe substitutes pork but maintains the style of cooking.

> 30 MINUTES OR LESS
> FAMILY FRIENDLY

½ cup all-purpose flour

2 cups **bread crumbs**

2 **eggs**, lightly beaten

1 cup clarified butter, divided

4 **bone-in pork chops**

Salt

1. Put the flour in a small bowl and the bread crumbs in a separate bowl.

2. Working with one chop at a time, lightly coat each in the flour, then dip in the beaten eggs and then in the bread crumbs. Gently press the bread crumbs into the pork chops so that much of the coating sticks.

3. Put ½ cup of clarified butter into a large skillet over medium-low heat. Working in two batches, heat the butter and add two chops. Cook on one side for 7 to 8 minutes, then flip and cook an additional 7 to 8 minutes until fully cooked. Add the remaining ½ cup of butter and repeat with the other two chops. Serve immediately.

For Your Next Visit: Ready to try an authentic cotoletta alla Milanese in Milan? Head to da Martino on Via Carlo Farini, Milan. They've been serving this specialty since 1950.

POLLO
Chicken

CHICKEN WITH PEPPERS / *Peperonata di Pollo* **(Lazio)** 100

VENETIAN CHICKEN / *Pollo alla Veneziana* **(Veneto)** 101

JUMP-IN-YOUR-MOUTH CHICKEN / *Saltimbocca alla Romana* **(Lazio)** 103

LEMON CAPER CHICKEN / *Pollo con Capperi e Limone* **(Sardinia)** 104

SICILIAN-STYLE CHICKEN / *Pollo alla Siciliana* **(Sicily)** 105

CHICKEN IN RED SAUCE / *Pollo al Sugo Rosso* **(Friuli–Venezia Giulia)** 106

ROASTED CALABRIAN CHICKEN / *Pollo al Forno Calabrese* **(Calabria)** 107

CHICKEN MARSALA / *Pollo Marsala* **(Sicily)** 108

PAN CHICKEN WITH TOMATO / *Pollo alla Pizzaiola* **(Campania)** 109

CHICKEN BREASTS WITH BALSAMIC GLAZE / *Pollo al Balsamico* **(Emilia-Romagna)** 110

CHICKEN IN WHITE WINE / *Bocconcini di Pollo al Vino Bianco* **(Friuli–Venezia Giulia)** 111

CHICKEN BUNDLES / *Involtini di Pollo* **(Emilia-Romagna)** 112

VALDOSTANA CUTLET / *Cotoletta Valdostana* **(Valle D'Aosta)** 113

Chicken is used extensively in Italy as a quick second course and is especially enjoyed by youngsters when it's fried up in cutlets. Prepared in countless ways, chicken is a great conductor of flavor, quickly absorbing the essence of what it's cooked in, whether that be wine, tomato sauce, butter, or oil. Boneless chicken is ideal for stovetop cooking, and bone-in cuts are a great option for oven cooking.

CHICKEN WITH PEPPERS
Peperonata di Pollo

PREP TIME: 10 MINUTES // **COOK TIME:** 25 MINUTES // **YIELD:** 4 SERVINGS

Lean, delicious, and versatile, chicken is not only a go-to for many home cooks in Italy, but it is also very frequently served in Italian restaurants as a second course. This particular dish is rustic and flavorful and ideal for anyone wanting to eat light but not skimp on flavor. This dish is a favorite served at the *trattorie* (eateries) in Lazio, especially in the area of the *Castelli Romani*, or Roman Castles.

> KID FRIENDLY
> FAMILY FRIENDLY
> DAIRY FREE

¼ cup olive oil, divided

3 skinless boneless chicken breasts, thinly cut into strips

½ cup white wine

4 red bell peppers, cut into ¼-inch strips

1 medium onion, chopped

3 garlic cloves, finely minced

1 tablespoon chopped fresh parsley

1 teaspoon dried oregano

Salt

1. In a large sauté pan over low to medium heat, heat 2 tablespoons of oil. Add the chicken and fry until it has taken on some color on all sides.

2. Add the wine and let it cook down for 1 to 2 minutes.

3. Add the bell peppers, onion, garlic, parsley, oregano, remaining 2 tablespoons of oil, and salt, and mix well.

4. Cook uncovered on medium-low heat for 20 minutes. If the chicken is drying up too quickly, add a few tablespoons of water. Serve immediately.

Substitution Tip: *For speed and efficiency, this recipe uses thin strips of chicken breasts, but bone-in chicken pieces such as thighs or drumsticks also work wonderfully. Adjust the cooking time accordingly—bone-in pieces will take longer to cook.*

VENETIAN CHICKEN
Pollo alla Veneziana

PREP TIME: 10 MINUTES // **COOK TIME:** 20 MINUTES // **YIELD:** 4 SERVINGS

Fegato alla Veneziana is a traditional Venetian dish that consists of veal liver, lots of onions, and white wine. It's served in casual restaurants and many homes, but we recognize that it's not something many in the United States would appreciate. So, in this recipe, I've maintained the cooking style and other ingredients but have changed the protein to chicken, which is generally better received.

> 30 MINUTES OR LESS
> KID FRIENDLY
> FAMILY FRIENDLY

1 tablespoon butter

3 tablespoons olive oil

2 small onions, sliced

Salt

Freshly ground black pepper

2 tablespoons water

4 or 5 sage leaves, chopped

1 tablespoon white wine vinegar

4 thin chicken breast cutlets, pounded to ⅛-inch thickness

1. In a large skillet over low heat, heat the butter and oil until the butter is melted. Add the onions, salt and pepper to taste, and water. Cook for 5 minutes, then add the sage and vinegar.

2. Continue cooking the onions with the vinegar, stirring occasionally, until they are almost fully cooked.

3. Add the chicken and increase the heat to medium. Continue cooking until the chicken is no longer pink, about 12 minutes, turning a few times during the process.

For Your Next Visit: *If you are headed to Venice, stop by Osteria al Cicheto, Cannaregio 367/A, and try the original Venetian dish. They add figs to theirs!*

JUMP-IN-YOUR-MOUTH CHICKEN
Saltimbocca alla Romana

PREP TIME: 10 MINUTES // **COOK TIME:** 20 MINUTES // **YIELD:** 4 SERVINGS

The recipe for traditional *Saltimbocca alla Romana* used veal cutlets, but it's very acceptable these days to substitute chicken or even thin turkey cutlets. Enhanced by the flavor and saltiness of the prosciutto, this recipe is surprisingly simple to prepare. The term "saltimbocca" translates to "jump in your mouth," and it is believed that the deliciousness of this dish is so extraordinary that it will literally jump in your mouth!

> 30 MINUTES OR LESS
> KID FRIENDLY
> FAMILY FRIENDLY

4 thin **chicken breast cutlets**, lightly pounded to ⅛-inch thickness

Salt

8 large **sage leaves**

4 thin slices **prosciutto**

½ cup all-purpose flour

3 tablespoons olive oil

4 tablespoons butter, divided

¾ cup **chicken stock**

1. Lightly season the chicken with salt. Place 2 sage leaves on each of the chicken breasts. Lay a slice of prosciutto over the sage. Although not required, you may stitch the prosciutto and sage into the chicken with a toothpick.

2. Place the flour in a bowl, and dredge the chicken cutlets, shaking off any excess.

3. Combine the oil and 2 tablespoons of butter in a large skillet over medium heat. Add the chicken breasts, prosciutto-side down, and cook until nearly cooked through, about 10 minutes. Flip the chicken and cook an additional 2 minutes. Transfer the chicken to a plate.

4. Add the remaining 2 tablespoons of butter to the skillet. Add the chicken stock and bring it to a boil. Cook until reduced by half, about 3 minutes.

5. Return the chicken to the skillet and simmer over medium heat for an additional 2 minutes. Transfer the chicken to plates, remove the toothpicks (if using), and pour the sauce on top.

Wine Pairing: *A fruity rosé will pair nicely with the saltiness of this dish. Try Donna Rosa Rosato, produced in my native region of Calabria.*

LEMON CAPER CHICKEN
Pollo con Capperi e Limone

PREP TIME: 10 MINUTES // **COOK TIME:** 15 MINUTES // **YIELD:** 4 SERVINGS

Capers have always symbolized the town of Selargius, near Cagliari in Sardinia. Old caper bushes that were once abandoned have been revitalized by new cultivators, and now close to 4,500 pounds of capers from nearly 50,000 caper plants grow here. Believed to have healing properties, capers commonly make their way into Sardinian cooking. Capers and lemon pair very well together, and both are key ingredients in this dish.

> 30 MINUTES OR LESS
> FAMILY FRIENDLY
> DAIRY FREE

4 thin **chicken breast cutlets**, lightly pounded to ⅛-inch thickness

Salt

Freshly ground black pepper

½ cup all-purpose flour

2 tablespoons olive oil

1 sprig **rosemary**, leaves only

Juice of 1 **lemon**

3 tablespoons **capers**, rinsed (see tip)

1. Season the chicken cutlets with salt and pepper.

2. Place the flour in a bowl and lightly dredge the chicken cutlets, dusting off any excess, and set aside.

3. In a small frying pan over medium heat, heat the oil for 1 to 2 minutes. Add the chicken, rosemary, and lemon juice.

4. Cook the chicken for 5 to 6 minutes per side, depending on thickness. During the last minute of cooking, add the capers. Plate and serve immediately.

Prep Tip: *Capers add saltiness to all dishes, so you may or may not wish to rinse them before adding them to a recipe. Adjust other additions of salt accordingly when preparing any dish that uses capers.*

SICILIAN-STYLE CHICKEN
Pollo alla Siciliana

PREP TIME: 10 MINUTES // **COOK TIME:** 25 MINUTES // **YIELD:** 4 SERVINGS

A visit to Sicily might lead you to believe that every dish originating from this region has olives in it! With thousands of miles of perfectly groomed olive trees, their fruit starts to show around May and locals cultivate their harvest in early November. If you're visiting Sicily during this period, you're likely to notice the smell of olive oil being pressed at the local mills. We use chicken tenders in this recipe, but any form of chicken will do; just adjust your cooking time accordingly.

> FAMILY FRIENDLY
> DAIRY FREE

3 tablespoons olive oil

1 garlic clove, minced

Red pepper flakes

1½ pounds chicken tenders

1 pint cherry tomatoes, halved

1 cup olives, pitted and halved

3 tablespoons capers, rinsed
   if desired

Salt

1 cup dry white wine

1 cup water

1. In a large sauté pan over medium heat, combine the oil, garlic, and red pepper flakes. Heat for 1 minute while stirring gently with a wooden spoon so the garlic does not burn.

2. Add the chicken and brown on all sides. Add the cherry tomatoes, olives, capers, and salt to taste.

3. Add the wine and let it evaporate, then add the water, reduce the heat to low, cover, and cook for 20 minutes until the tenders are fully cooked.

Substitution Tip: While fresh cherry tomatoes are typically used in this recipe, you can swap them out for canned whole tomatoes. Using canned tomatoes will give you a saucier, but no less delicious, final dish.

CHICKEN IN RED SAUCE
Pollo al Sugo Rosso

PREP TIME: 10 MINUTES // **COOK TIME:** 30 MINUTES // **YIELD:** 4 SERVINGS

Due to its geographic location, Friuli–Venezia Giulia leans toward a cuisine that mostly focuses on resources from the land as opposed to the sea. Its cuisine is simple, genuine, authentic, and without excess, especially when compared to other local regions that focus on heavier, buttery sauces. It is also heavily influenced by Austria, to which this region once belonged. The meat in this dish makes a wonderful second course, and dressing the pasta with the sauce turns this into a one-recipe, two-course meal.

> FAMILY FRIENDLY
> DAIRY FREE

3 tablespoons olive oil

½ small onion, diced

2 tablespoons chopped fresh parsley

1 teaspoon salt

2 garlic cloves, roughly chopped

8 chicken thighs, skin removed (or other chicken pieces of your choice)

1 (28-ounce) can crushed tomatoes

1¼ cups water, plus more if needed

1. In a medium saucepan over medium heat, combine the oil, onion, and parsley, and simmer for a few minutes. Add the salt and garlic, and stir.

2. Add the chicken and brown on all sides.

3. Add the tomatoes and water, reduce the heat to low, cover, and let simmer for 30 minutes, checking every 10 minutes or so to make sure it is not sticking to the pan. If the sauce is drying up, add an additional ½ cup of water.

Substitution Tip: *For even faster cooking, you can use chicken tenders in this dish. Tenders are also leaner than chicken thighs.*

ROASTED CALABRIAN CHICKEN
Pollo al Forno Calabrese

PREP TIME: 10 MINUTES // **COOK TIME:** 30 MINUTES // **YIELD:** 4 SERVINGS

Known for tomatoes, red onions, peppers, and potatoes, Calabria's cuisine is rustic, and the people really abide by shopping and eating local, so they prefer to make use of what grows closest to them. This classic dish is served in local casual *trattorie* (eateries), as well as prepared at home during the cold winter months, when roasting in a hot oven is a welcomed mode of cooking.

> KID FRIENDLY
> FAMILY FRIENDLY
> DAIRY FREE

Nonstick cooking spray

8 boneless skinless chicken thighs

1 teaspoon salt

1 small onion, sliced

3 tablespoons olive oil

2 or 3 sprigs rosemary, leaves only

2 to 3 teaspoons dried oregano

2 or 3 medium potatoes, peeled and cubed

1 lemon, halved

1. Preheat the oven to 375°F, and move the oven rack to the second-lowest position. Coat a baking sheet with cooking spray or a few additional tablespoons of oil.

2. In a large mixing bowl, combine the chicken thighs, salt, onion, oil, rosemary, oregano, and potatoes, and mix well using clean hands or two wooden spoons.

3. Squeeze the lemon over all the ingredients.

4. Spread the ingredients on the baking sheet, and bake until the chicken is fully cooked, about 30 minutes.

Ingredient Tip: *Running low on time? Why not scrub your potatoes clean and keep the skin on? Absorbing all the flavors and herbs, skin-on potatoes are delicious and offer more fiber than the peeled ones.*

CHICKEN MARSALA
Pollo Marsala

PREP TIME: 10 MINUTES // **COOK TIME:** 15 MINUTES // **YIELD:** 4 SERVINGS

A classic restaurant dish both in Italy and the United States, this recipe is so easy to prepare that it's no wonder it's becoming a popular home-cooked dish. It contains just a few simple ingredients and steps, so it comes together quickly, thanks in part to the cut of chicken selected. Marsala is a brandy-fortified wine from the Sicilian town of Marsala. It's a bit sweet and is used in savory dishes as well as desserts.

> 30 MINUTES OR LESS
> FAMILY FRIENDLY
> DAIRY FREE

4 thin chicken cutlets, pounded to ⅛-inch thickness

Salt

Freshly ground black pepper

½ cup all-purpose flour

3 tablespoons olive oil

8 ounces button mushrooms, sliced

¾ cup Marsala wine

¼ cup low-sodium chicken stock

1. Sprinkle the chicken with salt and pepper on both sides, and lightly dredge in the flour, shaking off the excess.

2. In a large sauté pan over medium heat, heat the oil. Fry the chicken until golden, 7 to 9 minutes, turning it a few times to brown on both sides. Remove from the pan and set aside.

3. Add the mushrooms to the pan and sauté for 5 minutes.

4. Pour in the Marsala wine and cook down for a few minutes. Add the stock and bring the mixture to a boil. Return the chicken to the pan, and simmer for a few minutes to allow the sauce to thicken to your desired consistency.

5. Plate the chicken and top with the sauce and mushrooms.

Substitution Tip: Turkey cutlets are also wonderful in this dish. Pound them to about ⅛-inch thickness before preparing.

PAN CHICKEN WITH TOMATO
Pollo alla Pizzaiola

PREP TIME: 5 MINUTES // **COOK TIME:** 15 MINUTES // **YIELD:** 4 SERVINGS

Cooking "*alla pizzaiola*" implies the use of tomatoes and frequently some oregano. These are the ingredients typically found on pizza; as such, this term was coined to represent any meat or even seafood that uses these ingredients in the recipe. This is a Neapolitan method of cooking, and while this particular recipe calls for chicken, you can just as easily swap in veal, beef, or even some sausages.

> 30 MINUTES OR LESS
> KID FRIENDLY
> FAMILY FRIENDLY
> DAIRY FREE

3 tablespoons olive oil

2 garlic cloves, minced

1 pint cherry tomatoes, halved

1 teaspoon salt

1 pound chicken tenders, cut into 4 or 5 pieces

1 teaspoon dried oregano

¼ cup black or green olives, pitted

1. In a large sauté pan over low heat, combine the oil and garlic, and cook for one minute. Add the tomatoes and salt, increase the heat to medium, and cook the tomatoes until they burst and cook down, about 5 minutes.

2. Add the chicken and oregano to the pan, mixing well. Add the olives.

3. Continue cooking until the chicken is no longer pink, about 10 additional minutes.

Substitution Tip: Fresh cherry tomatoes offer liveliness to this dish, but if you are looking to dress some pasta with the sauce and turn this recipe into a two-course meal, use 2 cups of canned crushed tomatoes instead.

CHICKEN BREASTS WITH BALSAMIC GLAZE
Pollo al Balsamico

PREP TIME: 10 MINUTES // **COOK TIME:** 30 MINUTES // **YIELD:** 4 SERVINGS

While traditional balsamic vinegar of Modena is highly praised, it's also regulated by the Italian government and comes with a price tag to match its elite status. However, the everyday variety is wonderful for dressing salads and making marinades. It adds sweetness to dishes and is used throughout Italy in various meat courses. Keep a bottle in your pantry, as you will get much use out of it.

> KID FRIENDLY
> FAMILY FRIENDLY
> DAIRY FREE

1 small onion, quartered

3 garlic cloves

Several sprigs parsley, stemmed

1 carrot, chopped

½ cup balsamic vinegar

¼ cup olive oil

1 teaspoon dried oregano

Salt

Freshly ground black pepper

4 medium boneless chicken breasts

1. Preheat the oven to 375°F.

2. In a food processor, combine the onion, garlic, parsley, and carrot, and pulse for 1 minute. Add the vinegar, oil, oregano, season with salt and pepper, and pulse for several minutes until a thick marinade is formed.

3. Place the chicken in a baking dish. Using a pastry brush, coat the chicken with half the marinade. Reserve the remaining marinade.

4. Bake the chicken for 30 minutes, adding the rest of the marinade halfway through the cooking time.

5. Slice the chicken breasts and serve immediately.

Substitution Tip: *This marinade is also wonderful on steak tips and pork loins.*

CHICKEN IN WHITE WINE
Bocconcini di Pollo al Vino Bianco

PREP TIME: 5 MINUTES // **COOK TIME:** 15 MINUTES // **YIELD:** 4 SERVINGS

Bocconcini translates to "little bites," and the term can be used to refer to little bites of chicken, mozzarella, chocolate-covered gelato, or whatever else requires just a bite or two to finish off. Since there are only a few ingredients in this dish, the flavor of the wine will really come through, so select a bottle that is flavorful enough to also drink.

> 30 MINUTES OR LESS
> DAIRY FREE

¼ cup olive oil

1 whole garlic clove

3 large **boneless chicken breasts**, cubed

½ cup all-purpose flour

1 cup **dry white wine**

1 sprig **rosemary**, leaves only

Salt

Freshly ground black pepper

1. In a medium sauté pan over low heat, combine the oil and garlic clove and allow the garlic to flavor the oil and turn golden, without burning.

2. Gently dust the chicken pieces with the flour, shaking off any excess. Remove the garlic clove, and add the chicken and wine to the pan. Increase the heat to medium. Add the rosemary, season with salt and pepper, and allow the chicken to cook in the wine and the alcohol to evaporate fully, 10 to 15 minutes, depending on the size of the chicken cubes. If the wine is drying up too quickly as it cooks, add a few tablespoons of water. Serve immediately.

Prep Tip: This dish cooks very quickly, so a great idea would be to prep the chicken in the morning by dusting with the flour, then refrigerating it. When you get home from work, you can just cook it with the rest of the ingredients.

CHICKEN BUNDLES
Involtini di Pollo

PREP TIME: 15 MINUTES // **COOK TIME:** 30 MINUTES // **YIELD:** 4 SERVINGS

Braciole (as we learned on page 87) simply refers to any dish that is rolled up into bundles, be it chicken, veal, or even thin slices of zucchini or eggplant. In this dish, we prepare chicken braciole, using the delicious prosciutto di Parma from the Emilia-Romagna region. Prosciutto adds a bit of saltiness and lots of flavor to any dish and makes a great stuffing for dishes such as this, as well as for stuffed pastas or sauces.

> KID FRIENDLY
> FAMILY FRIENDLY

8 thin chicken cutlets,
  pounded to ⅛-inch thickness
Salt
Freshly ground black pepper
8 slices prosciutto
8 slices provolone cheese
8 slices Italian salami
2 tablespoons butter
2 tablespoons olive oil
1 tablespoon chopped
  fresh parsley

1. Preheat the oven to 375°F.

2. Line up all the chicken cutlets on a sheet of wax paper, and season both sides with salt and pepper.

3. On each cutlet, place one slice each of prosciutto, provolone cheese, and salami, folding the ingredients in half if they are too large. Roll up the chicken as if rolling up a jellyroll. Secure with a toothpick and set aside.

4. In a large oven-safe sauté pan, melt the butter and add the oil. Add the parsley and the chicken bundles. Brown on all sides for several minutes.

5. After the chicken has browned, place the pan with the bundles in the oven to finish cooking, about 25 minutes. Be sure to remove the toothpicks before plating and serving.

Prep Tip: Serving these for a dinner party? Prepare them up to 8 hours in advance and simply refrigerate until ready to cook.

VALDOSTANA CUTLET
Cotoletta Valdostana

PREP TIME: 10 MINUTES // **COOK TIME:** 10 MINUTES // **YIELD:** 4 SERVINGS

The *Valdostana* cutlet is an indulgent and flavorful second course prominent in the region of Valle D'Aosta. Coated in a golden layer of crispy bread crumbs, the ingredients are few but important in obtaining a delicious cutlet that is crispy on the outside and filled with melted cheese on the inside. Traditionally made with veal, this recipe substitutes very thin chicken breasts and maintains the same cooking method.

> 30 MINUTES OR LESS
> KID FRIENDLY
> FAMILY FRIENDLY

¾ cup **bread crumbs**

8 very thin **chicken cutlets,** lightly pounded

¼ pound **deli-style ham**

¼ pound sliced **fontina cheese**

2 **eggs,** lightly beaten

Olive oil, for frying

Salt

Freshly ground black pepper

1. Put the bread crumbs in a bowl.

2. On four of the cutlets, place a folded slice of ham and a folded slice of cheese. Cover each with another cutlet, to make four packets in all.

3. Holding a packet at the seams, dip both sides in the egg, then in the bread crumbs. Place on a clean dish and repeat the process until all four packets are coated.

4. In a sauté pan over medium heat, heat 1 to 2 inches of oil until shimmering. Working in batches of two, carefully drop the cutlets into the oil, making sure the oil touches the seams to seal the two pieces of chicken together. Cook on one side until browned, then carefully turn the cutlets over and cook on the other side.

5. Remove from the oil and add salt and pepper to taste. Repeat with the remaining two packets.

Prep Tip: *If you are serving Cotolette Valdostana at your next dinner party, you can prep these a few hours in advance and refrigerate them until you're ready to fry.*

PESCE E FRUTTI DI MARE
Fish and Seafood

MUSSELS IN WINE AND RED SAUCE / *Cozze alla Tarantina* **(Puglia)** 117

COD IN BROTH / *Baccalà alla Trentina* **(Trentino–Alto Adige)** 118

SICILIAN SWORDFISH / *Pesce Spada alla Siciliana* **(Sicily)** 119

SWORDFISH IN RED SAUCE / *Pesce Spada in Salsa Rossa* **(Sicily)** 120

SWEET AND SOUR SWORDFISH / *Pesce Spada in Agrodolce* **(Sicily)** 121

COD WITH POTATOES / *Baccalà con Patate* **(Calabria)** 122

TRIESTE-STYLE COD / *Baccalà alla Triestina* **(Friuli–Venezia Giulia)** 123

CLAMS IN BROTH / *Vongole in Umido* **(Sardinia)** 124

TROUT IN FOIL / *Trota al Cartoccio* **(Puglia)** 125

DEVILED SHRIMP / *Scampi Indiavolati* **(Calabria)** 126

SCALLOPS WITH GARLIC AND CAPERS / *Scaloppine Profumate* **(Puglia)** 127

MEDITERRANEAN-STYLE SALMON /
Filetti di Salmone alla Mediterrania **(Southern Italy)** 128

Eaten at least once or twice a week in Italy, fish is steadily increasing in popularity. It's served frequently as a second course, after pasta or risotto, or in some form of sauce added to pasta. Italians enjoy seafood for good reason. Since the nation is surrounded by several seas, the freshness and availability is unmatched. Be it sturdy fish, such as swordfish or cod, or the ever-popular mussels and clams, the Italian repertoire for seafood is vast and delicious. Seafood cooks quickly and absorbs flavor wonderfully, making it ideal for a quick dinner. Garlic, oregano, and tomatoes are a consistent presence in Italian seafood dishes.

MUSSELS IN WINE AND RED SAUCE
Cozze alla Tarantina

PREP TIME: 10 MINUTES // **COOK TIME:** 15 MINUTES // **YIELD:** 4 SERVINGS

Famous for sun, sand, and sea, the region of Puglia is abundant in seafood. Recipes from Puglia, like this one, are spicy, rustic, and adored for their simplicity. This recipe was once considered part of the *cucina povera*, or "poor man's cooking" concept. Not so today, as the costs of the ingredients used have increased. This recipe is part soup, part sauce, and complete deliciousness.

> 30 MINUTES OR LESS
> GLUTEN FREE
> DAIRY FREE

4 tablespoons olive oil, divided

4 garlic cloves, minced, divided

¾ cup dry white wine

2 pounds mussels, scrubbed and debearded

1 (14-ounce) can canned tomatoes

Red pepper flakes

Salt

Freshly ground black pepper

1 tablespoon chopped fresh parsley

1. In a medium pan over medium heat, combine 2 tablespoons of oil and half the garlic, and heat for 1 minute. Add the white wine and mussels, mix well, cover, and cook for about 5 minutes until the mussels open up. Discard any mussels that do not open. Strain the mussels, reserving the liquid.

2. Meanwhile, in a large sauté pan over medium heat, heat the remaining 2 tablespoons of olive oil and remaining garlic. Add the tomatoes and the broth from the mussels and cook for 10 minutes.

3. Add the mussels and red pepper flakes, season with salt and pepper, and simmer, covered, for an additional 5 minutes. Garnish with the parsley before serving.

Ingredient Tip: *Turn this recipe into a two-course meal by cooking some pasta and dressing it with the sauce from the mussels.*

COD IN BROTH
Baccalà alla Trentina

PREP TIME: 15 MINUTES // **COOK TIME:** 20 MINUTES // **YIELD:** 4 SERVINGS

A historic and typical recipe of Trentino–Alto Adige, this dish typically calls for salted cod that has been reconstituted in water for several days before preparing. Prepared at home as well as served in many restaurants, the traditional recipe can be labor intensive and time consuming, so this recipe modifies it slightly and uses cod loins, which has many similarities to salted cod and is readily available at most major markets in the United States.

> GLUTEN FREE

1 tablespoon butter

3 tablespoons olive oil

1 garlic clove

1½ pounds cod loins, cut into large chunks

2 medium potatoes, peeled and diced into 1-inch cubes

2 tablespoons chopped fresh parsley

1 to 1½ cups whole milk

Salt

Freshly ground black pepper

1. In a large sauté pan over low heat, heat the butter and oil slightly, and add the whole garlic clove.

2. Add the cod, potatoes, parsley, and enough milk to cover all the ingredients.

3. Seson with salt and pepper, and cook for about 20 minutes on low heat, stirring very gently during the cooking process, making sure not to overcook the fish or break it up. Remove the garlic before serving.

For Your Next Visit: *Headed to Trentino-Alto Adige? Why not stop at Ristorante Novecento in Hotel Rovereto, where this dish was born?*

SICILIAN SWORDFISH
Pesce Spada alla Siciliana

PREP TIME: 10 MINUTES // **COOK TIME:** 20 MINUTES // **YIELD:** 4 SERVINGS

Sicily, and all of southern Italy, is synonymous with swordfish. Swordfish is eaten far more frequently there than in the United States, and it's locally caught. That said, there really isn't one true recipe for what we are calling "Sicilian Swordfish." Every household has its own version, and you're unlikely to dine at two restaurants and find swordfish cooked the same way. In our recipe, we're using standard Sicilian ingredients such as olives, cherry tomatoes, and pine nuts.

> 30 MINUTES OR LESS
> FAMILY FRIENDLY
> GLUTEN FREE
> DAIRY FREE

3 tablespoons olive oil

1 garlic clove, halved

1 pint cherry tomatoes, halved

1 teaspoon dried oregano

Salt

½ cup black olives, pitted and halved

1½ pounds swordfish, cut into chunks

¼ cup toasted pine nuts

1. In a large sauté pan over low heat, warm the oil and garlic for a few minutes, being careful not to burn the garlic. Add the tomatoes and oregano, season with salt, and simmer for 5 minutes.

2. Remove and discard the garlic. Add the olives and swordfish, increase the heat to medium, cover, and cook for 5 to 6 minutes without turning. Flip the swordfish over and cook an additional 5 to 6 minutes, depending on the thickness of the swordfish pieces and your preferred doneness.

3. Plate the swordfish, topping it with the tomatoes. Add the pine nuts just before serving.

Substitution Tip: Make this recipe your own by substituting the olives and pine nuts for other typical Sicilian ingredients such as capers, raisins, anchovies, or diced zucchini and eggplant.

SWORDFISH IN RED SAUCE
Pesce Spada in Salsa Rossa

PREP TIME: 5 MINUTES // **COOK TIME:** 25 MINUTES // **YIELD:** 4 TO 6 SERVINGS

One of the largest islands in the Mediterranean, Sicily boasts a robust cuisine that is unique from that of the mainland. The scent of the ocean is present in many dishes, where health and well-being on a plate are celebrated. This dish is frequently made with cherry tomatoes; however, by using canned crushed tomatoes, as recommended here, you will end up with a lovely sauce that's also ideal for dressing some pasta.

> 30 MINUTES OR LESS
> GLUTEN FREE
> DAIRY FREE

3 tablespoons olive oil

½ medium onion, diced

2 tablespoons chopped fresh parsley

3 garlic cloves, halved

1 teaspoon salt

1½ pounds swordfish, cut into large chunks

1 (28-ounce) can crushed tomatoes

1 cup water

1. In a large sauté pan over low heat, heat the oil, onion, parsley, garlic, and salt, and simmer for a few minutes, making sure the garlic does not burn.

2. Add the swordfish and allow it to brown for several minutes on each side. Remove and discard the garlic pieces.

3. Add the tomatoes and water, and simmer, uncovered, for 20 minutes, stirring a few times during the cooking process.

For Your Next Visit: Headed to Sicily? Be sure to visit Al Saraceno in Taormina. With magnificent views, the seafood options can't be beat.

SWEET AND SOUR SWORDFISH
Pesce Spada in Agrodolce

PREP TIME: 15 MINUTES // **COOK TIME:** 15 MINUTES // **YIELD:** 4 SERVINGS

Agrodolce means "bittersweet" in Italian, and this recipe from Sicily fits the bill. The sweetness from the red onions paired with the vinegar offers a flavorful, relish-like topping that is juicy and delicious on top of some plainly pan-fried swordfish. While I often use white and red onions interchangeably, for this recipe, I recommend red onions for their unique sweetness—they work wonderfully in this dish.

> 30 MINUTES OR LESS
> GLUTEN FREE
> DAIRY FREE

1 cup water

2 tablespoons white wine vinegar

1 tablespoon sugar

3 tablespoons olive oil, divided

4 small or medium red onions, thinly sliced

Salt

Freshly ground black pepper

2 garlic cloves, minced

4 swordfish steaks

2 teaspoons dried oregano

1. In a small bowl, mix the water, vinegar, and sugar. Set aside.

2. In a sauté pan over medium heat, combine 2 tablespoons of oil and the onions, and sauté them for 2 minutes. Add the water mixture, season with salt and pepper, cover, and cook the onions for 10 to 15 minutes more.

3. In the meantime, in a separate pan over low heat, heat the remaining 1 tablespoon of oil and the garlic and simmer briefly. Add the swordfish, season with salt and pepper, and cook for 5 to 6 minutes per side, or longer if preferred.

4. Plate the swordfish and top each steak with the sweetened onions. Sprinkle with the oregano.

Ingredient Tip: Did you know that the relish created for topping this swordfish is also delicious as a topping on pizza dough or focaccia? Prepare the crust and top with this delicious add-on.

COD WITH POTATOES
Baccalà con Patate

PREP TIME: 15 MINUTES // **COOK TIME:** 30 MINUTES // **YIELD:** 4 SERVINGS

Growing up in Calabria, I recall my family preparing this dish very regularly, especially during the winter holidays. We would use salted cod, which required at least three days of soaking and frequent water changes. This is done in order to remove the salt used in curing it. As is typical of home recipes, every family has their own version. Once we moved to the United States, we began using cod loins, as they are much more common and convenient.

> FAMILY FRIENDLY
> GLUTEN FREE
> DAIRY FREE

3 tablespoons olive oil

2 or 3 garlic cloves, sliced

2 to 3 tablespoons chopped fresh parsley

1 teaspoon dried oregano

2 cups canned crushed tomatoes

3 medium potatoes, peeled and diced

2 cups water, divided

Salt

1½ pounds cod loins

1. In a large sauté pan over medium heat, combine the oil, garlic, and parsley. Cook for about 1 minute, just long enough to heat up the oil.

2. Add the oregano and tomatoes and cook for 5 minutes.

3. Add the potatoes and 1 cup of water, and cook for an additional 5 minutes. Add salt to taste.

4. Add the cod loins to the pan with the remaining 1 cup of water. Simmer, uncovered, for 20 minutes, until the broth has thickened. Serve with crusty bread or pasta.

Substitution Tip: *Haddock works just as wonderfully in this recipe and provides a very similar flavor.*

TRIESTE-STYLE COD
Baccalà alla Triestina

PREP TIME: 15 MINUTES // **COOK TIME:** 40 MINUTES // **YIELD:** 4 TO 6 SERVINGS

Traditionally made with salted cod that has been rehydrated, this classic recipe from the town of Trieste in Friuli–Venezia Giulia can be made *bianca* (without red sauce) or *rossa* (with red sauce). This is the bianca recipe (see tip for rossa). While delicious, salted cod can be labor intensive, requires three to four days of soaking in water, and can be hard to find in the United States. In this recipe, we use cod loins, which are similar in style, taste, and texture.

> GLUTEN FREE

> DAIRY FREE

3 tablespoons olive oil, plus more for drizzling

2 pounds potatoes, peeled and cut into thin slices resembling potato chips

Salt

Freshly ground black pepper

12 canned anchovies, chopped

2 tablespoons chopped fresh parsley, plus more for sprinkling

1½ pounds cod loins, cut into chunks

1 cup water

1. Preheat the oven to 375°F.

2. Pour the oil into a baking dish. Add a layer of potatoes, sprinkle with salt and pepper, half of the anchovies, and half of the parsley.

3. Place half of the cod chunks over the potatoes, drizzle with oil, and repeat the layering, ending with a layer of potatoes.

4. Top the last layer of potatoes with an additional drizzle of oil and more parsley. Pour the water over the entire dish and bake for 40 minutes.

Substitution Tip: Want to make the red version? Add a ladleful of canned tomatoes between each layer of fish and potatoes, and skip the cup of water at the end.

CLAMS IN BROTH
Vongole in Umido

PREP TIME: 5 MINUTES // **COOK TIME:** 5 TO 7 MINUTES // **YIELD:** 4 SERVINGS

Served most frequently in *umido*, or broth, clams and mussels are very popular in southern Italy, and Sardinia is just one of the regions that prepares these delicious shellfish in a wine broth. The broth is mostly intended to dress some "long" pasta, such as spaghetti, or to be mopped up with some warm crusty bread. This method is a tasty and easy way to prepare seafood on a busy weeknight.

> 30 MINUTES OR LESS
> GLUTEN FREE
> DAIRY FREE

3 tablespoons olive oil

2 garlic cloves, minced

2 pounds clams, scrubbed clean

1 cup dry white wine

1 tablespoon chopped fresh parsley

1. In a large sauté pan over low heat, warm the oil and garlic for about 1 minute until the garlic has some color.

2. Add the clams and wine to the pan. Cover, increase the heat to medium, and cook until the clams open up, about 5 minutes. Discard any clams that do not open.

3. Remove the clams and sauce from the heat and dress with the parsley. Serve immediately over pasta or with some crusty bread.

Substitution Tip: *Mussels are a great substitution in this recipe. Just follow the steps as directed using mussels instead of clams.*

TROUT IN FOIL
Trota al Cartoccio

PREP TIME: 15 MINUTES // **COOK TIME:** 35 MINUTES // **YIELD:** 4 SERVINGS

Cooking *in cartoccio* basically means cooking in parchment paper. It's common in Italy to cook fish using this method, which essentially holds the moisture in and steams whatever is being cooked. It's also impressive to see guests open their packets and get a whiff of the beautiful aroma. In Puglia, "in cartoccio" is the preferred way of cooking trout.

> DAIRY FREE

½ cup plain bread crumbs

1 tablespoon finely chopped fresh parsley

2 garlic cloves, minced

1 lemon, zested and thinly sliced

2 tablespoons olive oil, plus more for drizzling

Salt

4 fresh rainbow trout, cleaned and deboned

2 medium potatoes, peeled and finely sliced

Freshly ground black pepper

1. Preheat the oven to 375°F.

2. Prepare the packets by cutting four large pieces each of aluminum foil and parchment paper. Place a piece of parchment paper on top of each piece of foil.

3. In a small container, make a stuffing by mixing the bread crumbs, parsley, garlic, lemon zest, and oil.

4. Sprinkle salt in the belly of the trout, and stuff with several slices each of potatoes and lemons, and about a tablespoon of bread stuffing.

5. Season the outside of the fish with salt and pepper, lightly drizzle oil on top, place a fish on each piece of parchment paper, and wrap them tightly in the premade wraps. Place the four fish packets on a baking sheet and bake for 30 to 35 minutes, depending on the size of the trout.

Substitution Tip: Any fish can be prepared al cartoccio, and some wonderful options include thick pieces of cod, swordfish, or even scallops.

DEVILED SHRIMP
Scampi Indiavolati

PREP TIME: 5 MINUTES // **COOK TIME:** 15 MINUTES // **YIELD:** 4 SERVINGS

Walking through the outdoor markets in Calabria, you will most definitely come across the typical *peperoncino rosso* that Calabria is known for. Often sold at outdoor markets, this miniscule pepper packs a big punch and can be used fresh or dry. Pasta is frequently topped with a wee bit of this pepper for added spice, and it's the main ingredient in deviled shrimp. In this recipe, we use red pepper flakes, which are readily available in the United States.

> 30 MINUTES OR LESS
> GLUTEN FREE
> DAIRY FREE

2 tablespoons olive oil

½ small onion, chopped

2 garlic cloves, minced

2 cups canned
  crushed tomatoes

Red pepper flakes

3 tablespoons chopped
  fresh parsley

½ cup water

1 pound medium shrimp,
  shelled and deveined

1. In a medium sauté pan over low heat, combine the oil and onion and cook, stirring occasionally, until the onion is translucent, 3 to 4 minutes.

2. Add the garlic, stirring to make sure it does not burn. Stir in the tomatoes, red pepper flakes to taste, parsley, and water. Increase the heat to medium and cook the sauce, uncovered, for 10 minutes.

3. Add the shrimp and cook them, stirring occasionally, until they turn pink, 4 to 5 minutes. Serve with pasta or with crusty bread.

Wine Pairing: *The heat of the pepper flakes may be too much with strong wines, so opt for a pinot grigio to complement the heat and tame it a bit.*

SCALLOPS WITH GARLIC AND CAPERS
Scaloppine Profumate

PREP TIME: 5 MINUTES // **COOK TIME:** 10 MINUTES // **YIELD:** 4 SERVINGS

Though this dish is traditionally served in a butter sauce, olive oil is the fat of choice in Puglia and all of southern Italy. As such, this dish is prepared using oil, wine, and lemon juice instead. Summery and light, sea scallops are an ideal weeknight meal because they cook quickly and absorb flavors very nicely. In this dish, I've added capers to heighten the southern Italian flavor.

> 30 MINUTES OR LESS
> FAMILY FRIENDLY
> GLUTEN FREE
> DAIRY FREE

3 tablespoons olive oil, divided

1 pound **scallops**, side muscle removed, rinsed

Salt

Freshly ground black pepper

¼ cup dry white wine

2 garlic cloves, minced

Juice of ½ **lemon**

2 tablespoons chopped fresh parsley

2 tablespoons **capers**, rinsed if desired

1. In a medium sauté pan over medium heat, heat 2 table-spoons of oil. Season the scallops with salt and pepper, and sear in the oil for 3 to 4 minutes per side until a light crust is formed. Remove the scallops from the pan and set aside.

2. In the same pan over low heat, add the remaining 1 tablespoon of oil, wine, garlic, lemon juice, and parsley, and heat, stirring constantly to ensure the garlic does not burn.

3. Return the scallops to the pan, add the capers, and allow all the flavors to blend, cooking for just a few minutes longer.

4. Serve over pasta, orzo, or rice, or alongside a green salad.

Wine Pairing: *Dry white wines pair well with scallops and most other seafood, so a nice Soave or Gavi will work wonderfully for both drinking and adding to the recipe.*

MEDITERRANEAN-STYLE SALMON
Filetti di Salmone alla Mediterrania

PREP TIME: 10 MINUTES, PLUS INACTIVE TIME // **COOK TIME:** 25 MINUTES // **YIELD:** 4 SERVINGS

It's amazing how prominent olives and capers are in southern Italian cuisine. When incorporated into seafood meals like this one, heavier sauces in the winter, or even pizza, these two ingredients add flavor, saltiness, and depth. Be sure to monitor additions of salt when cooking with these ingredients, as both add much salt on their own.

> FAMILY FRIENDLY
> GLUTEN FREE
> DAIRY FREE

1 pound cherry tomatoes, halved

¼ cup olive oil, plus more for baking dish

2 garlic cloves, halved

1 teaspoon dried oregano

½ teaspoon salt

4 salmon fillets

Salt

Freshly ground black pepper

½ cup black olives, pitted

2 tablespoons capers, rinsed

1. In a medium bowl, combine the tomatoes, oil, garlic, oregano, and salt, and mix well. Let stand for 20 minutes.

2. In the meantime, wash the salmon and remove any skin.

3. Preheat the oven to 375°F. Add a few tablespoons of oil to a baking dish. Spread the tomatoes in the dish and top with the salmon.

4. Season with salt and pepper. Add the olives and capers on top and bake for 20 to 25 minutes. During baking, scoop some of the tomatoes on top of the fish. Serve immediately.

Substitution Tip: *Cod, swordfish, haddock, or even scallops can easily be substituted in this recipe. Also, add parsley and basil for more flavor.*

DOLCE
Desserts

UGLY BUT GOOD / *Brutti ma Buoni* **(Piedmont)** 132

ANISE SPONGE / *Biscotti Soffici all'Anice* **(Southern Italy)** 133

RICCIARELLI / *Ricciarelli* **(Tuscany)** 134

TUSCAN CANTUCCI / *Cantucci di Toscana* **(Tuscany)** 135

WINE RINGS / *Tarallucci di Vino* **(Puglia)** 136

MOM'S "S" COOKIES / *Biscotti "S" di Mamma* **(Calabria)** 138

LEMON BUNDT / *Ciambella al Limone* **(Southern Italy)** 139

CAPRESE CAKE / *Torta Caprese* **(Campania)** 140

ZABAGLIONE / *Zabaglione* **(Sicily)** 142

CAT'S TONGUE COOKIES / *Lingue di Gatto* **(Trentino-Alto Adige)** 143

PIZZA WITH NUTELLA AND HAZELNUTS / *Pizza con Nutella e Nocciole* **(Piedmont)** 144

TIRAMISU / *Tiramisu* **(Veneto)** 145

LEMON SLUSH / *Lemon Granita* **(Sicily)** 148

Italy's la dolce vita is given a whole new meaning when it comes to Italian desserts. Italians love sweet endings, and in truth, even sweet beginnings! Mornings in Italy usually start with a *cornetto,* Italy's version of the croissant. For snacks at school, kids are often given a sweet treat, such as a piece of homemade *ciambella* (a citrus Bundt-style cake), or other homemade goodies. After dinner, dry biscotti such as *cantucci, brutti ma buoni*, or an anise cookie might be what ends the meal. Be it fancy or casual, a sweet treat to end a meal certainly makes it feel more complete.

UGLY BUT GOOD
Brutti ma Buoni

PREP TIME: 20 MINUTES // **COOK TIME:** 30 MINUTES // **YIELD:** 34 TO 36 COOKIES

It's rather unfortunate that these delicious and light meringue cookies have such an unsavory name, but *brutti ma buoni,* or "ugly but good," deserve a place on your cookie platter, despite their outward appearance. Believed to have originated from Piedmont, the largest hazelnut-growing region in Italy, these cookies contain just a few ingredients. Prepared in homes and also sold at many pastry shops, these Italian cookies are easy to make and very tasty. We'll add chopped chocolate to this version for an extra kick of sweetness.

> FAMILY FRIENDLY
> GLUTEN FREE

1½ cups toasted hazelnuts
1 cup granulated sugar, divided
Pinch salt
4 large egg whites
4 ounces dark chocolate,
　finely chopped

1. Preheat the oven to 300°F, and line two baking sheets with parchment paper. Set aside.

2. In a food processor, combine the hazelnuts, ¼ cup of sugar, and salt, and grind until the mixture resembles coarse bread crumbs.

3. Using a hand mixer or the whisk attachment on a stand mixer, whip the egg whites to soft peaks. While mixing, slowly add the remaining ¾ cup of sugar and continue whipping until stiff peaks form.

4. Gently fold the chopped nut mixture and chocolate into the egg whites until well incorporated. Using a 1½-inch cookie or ice cream scoop, scoop the cookies onto the prepared pans, spacing the cookies 2 inches apart. Bake for 25 to 30 minutes. Cool for 15 minutes before removing from the pan.

Wine Pairing: *These delicious treats are wonderful to end a meal. Pair them with some Vin Santo from Tuscany or Marsala wine from Sicily.*

ANISE SPONGE
Biscotti Soffici all'Anice

PREP TIME: 5 MINUTES // **COOK TIME:** 30 MINUTES // **YIELD:** ABOUT 20 COOKIES

In Italy, the term *biscotti* translates to all sorts of cookies and biscuits, and not just the hard, twice-baked version that's common in the United States. When it comes to traditional biscotti, there are literally hundreds of versions. Anise cookies offer a unique flavor, similar to licorice. These cookies are much softer than traditional ones and are nut-free, making them a favorite for nearly all palates.

> KID FRIENDLY
> FAMILY FRIENDLY
> DAIRY FREE

1 cup all-purpose flour
2 tablespoons cornstarch
1 teaspoon baking powder
¼ teaspoon table salt
2 large eggs
¾ cup sugar
2 teaspoons anise extract

1. Preheat the oven to 350°F, and line a baking sheet with parchment paper.

2. In a bowl, mix together the flour, cornstarch, baking powder, and salt.

3. With a mixer on high speed, beat the eggs and sugar together for several minutes. Mix in the anise extract.

4. With a rubber spatula, add the flour mixture and blend just until combined. The batter will be soft.

5. Pour the batter down the middle of the baking sheet so it will form a log. It will be too soft to handle with your hands. Bake for 20 minutes. Remove from the oven and cool for a few minutes.

6. Peel the parchment paper from the log. Slice the log into biscotti the size of your choosing. Return the biscotti, cut-side down, to the baking sheet, and bake for an additional 5 minutes. Turn them over and bake for an additional 5 minutes on the other side.

Substitution Tip: *While traditionally made with anise, several variations include vanilla, lemon, or orange extract.*

RICCIARELLI
Ricciarelli

PREP TIME: 20 MINUTES, PLUS INACTIVE TIME // **COOK TIME:** 20 MINUTES // **YIELD:** 22 TO 24 COOKIES

In Tuscany's almond-growing area of Siena, *ricciarelli* are enjoyed throughout the year, but particularly at Christmastime. Both soft and chewy, these macaroon-like biscuits are preferred among those following a gluten-free diet or looking for a treat without the guilt. These cookies are traditionally shaped into a diamond, so you can attempt to shape them with wet hands or simply just scoop some dough into small mounds instead.

> KID FRIENDLY
> FAMILY FRIENDLY
> GLUTEN FREE
> DAIRY FREE

2½ cups toasted slivered almonds

2 teaspoons orange zest

1 cup confectioners' sugar, divided, plus more for dusting the cookies

2 large egg whites

Pinch salt

1 teaspoon vanilla extract

1. Line two baking sheets with parchment paper. Set aside.

2. In the bowl of a food processor, combine the almonds, zest, and ½ cup of confectioners' sugar, and grind until the mixture resembles fine bread crumbs.

3. Use a hand mixer or stand mixer to mix the egg whites until soft peaks form. Gradually add the remaining ½ cup of sugar and salt, and continue mixing until stiff peaks form.

4. Fold the almond mixture and vanilla into the egg whites until combined. Drop a scoop of several tablespoons of the mixture onto the parchment paper, and with wet hands, construct a diamond shape. Repeat the process with the remaining batter. Let the cookies stand for at least 1 hour to dry out.

5. Preheat the oven to 350°F. Place the cookies on a baking sheet, about 1 inch apart, and bake for 15 to 20 minutes until the corners have darkened and the top is cracked. The center will be soft. Dust with confectioners' sugar.

Substitution Tip: If you don't have almonds, you can follow the exact same recipe using hazelnuts, pecans, or even peeled pistachios instead.

TUSCAN CANTUCCI
Cantucci di Toscana

PREP TIME: 15 MINUTES // **COOK TIME:** 35 TO 40 MINUTES // **YIELD:** 24 TO 30

Cantucci are twice-baked biscotti originating from the Tuscany region. Adored throughout Italy, these dry and hard cookies are rather humble, containing neither butter nor oil. However, they do not disappoint. Once you master this basic recipe, change it up a bit according to your liking.

> KID FRIENDLY

> FAMILY FRIENDLY

> DAIRY FREE

2 cups all-purpose flour

1 cup sugar

1 teaspoon baking powder

¼ teaspoon salt

2 large eggs plus 1 large egg yolk, lightly beaten

Zest of 1 large orange

1 cup hazelnuts or almonds, roughly chopped

1. Preheat the oven to 350°F. Line a baking sheet with parchment paper.

2. On a clean surface, mix the flour, sugar, baking powder, and salt by stirring with a fork.

3. Make a well in the middle, and add the eggs and zest. Using a fork or your fingers, start incorporating some of the flour into the egg, little by little, until a dough is formed.

4. Add the nuts and mix into the dough until well incorporated. Divide the dough in half and form two logs. Place them on the baking sheet several inches apart.

5. Bake for 22 to 25 minutes. Remove the logs from the oven and cool for 10 minutes. Using a serrated knife, cut the logs diagonally into slices, place them back on the baking sheet, cut-side down, lower the oven temperature to 325°F, and bake for 10 to 15 more minutes, turning halfway through so they toast evenly.

Wine Pairing: *In Tuscany, cantucci are typically soaked in some Vin Santo, so grab a glass for some dunking.*

WINE RINGS
Tarallucci di Vino

PREP TIME: 15 MINUTES, PLUS MORE FOR SHAPING // **COOK TIME:** 25 MINUTES // **YIELD:** 32 TO 38 COOKIES

Sweet or savory, soft or crispy, sugared or with black pepper, *taralli* are an institution in and of themselves in southern Italy—just about every household has its own version; in fact, each household likely has several versions. The savory kind is used as an appetizer, to be enjoyed with antipasti such as cubed cheese or olives. Sweet versions, such as this one, are enjoyed with a cup of espresso for breakfast or as an afternoon snack to tide one over until dinner.

> KID FRIENDLY
> FAMILY FRIENDLY
> DAIRY FREE

3½ cups all-purpose flour, plus more for shaping

2 teaspoons baking powder

¼ teaspoon salt

3 large eggs

1 cup granulated sugar, plus extra for dusting (optional)

½ cup light-tasting olive oil (see tip)

1 cup dry or sweet white wine

1. Preheat the oven to 350°F, and line two baking sheets with parchment paper.

2. In a bowl, sift together the flour, baking powder, and salt, and set aside.

3. In the bowl of a stand mixer or with a hand mixer, mix the eggs on high speed until light and creamy, 4 to 5 minutes. Add the sugar and continue mixing until combined.

4. On low speed, mix in the oil and wine until combined. Slowly add the flour mixture until well combined, without overbeating the dough. The dough will be relatively soft.

5. Scoop out a few tablespoons of dough, and with floured hands, roll into a 6- or 7-inch strand about a half inch in diameter. Shape the strand into a ring, and press the ends together to connect them. Repeat with the remaining dough. Sprinkle a bit of sugar on top, if desired. Bake the taralli for 22 to 25 minutes, or until golden.

Ingredient Tip: *There are olive oils on the market called "extra light-tasting olive oil" or "light-tasting olive oil." The taste is almost bland, and I recommend using it in baking when you don't want sweets to taste savory.*

Wine Pairing: *A sweet or sparkly white wine such as a Spumante from Asti will pair nicely with these little taralli.*

MOM'S "S" COOKIES
Biscotti "S" di Mamma

PREP TIME: 15 MINUTES, PLUS MORE FOR SHAPING // **COOK TIME:** 15 TO 20 MINUTES
// **YIELD:** 40 TO 60 COOKIES

During my childhood in Italy, my mom was a stay-at-home mom, and much of her time was spent cooking and baking for our family. Italians prefer cooking locally and regionally, so southern Italian treats such as these "S" cookies that my mom made regularly call for olive oil as opposed to butter. Because of the abundance of olive trees and oil in the region, many southern baked desserts call for oil as the fat of choice.

> KID FRIENDLY
> FAMILY FRIENDLY
> DAIRY FREE

4½ cups all-purpose flour

2 teaspoons baking powder

5 large eggs, divided

1 cup granulated sugar,
   plus extra for sprinkling
   the cookies

¾ cup light-tasting olive oil

Zest of 1 lemon or orange

1. Preheat the oven to 375°F. Line two or three baking sheets with parchment paper.

2. In a large bowl, whisk together the flour and baking powder.

3. Using a stand mixer or hand mixer, combine 4 eggs, sugar, oil, and zest. Mix just until all the ingredients are blended.

4. Slowly add in the flour mixture and beat on medium speed until a soft dough forms.

5. Pull off pieces of dough and roll out ropes about 1 inch thick and 5 to 7 inches long. Shape each rope into an "S" shape. Place on the lined baking sheets, about 2 inches apart.

6. In a small bowl, beat the remaining egg with a fork. Brush each cookie with the egg and sprinkle with a small pinch of sugar.

7. Bake for 15 to 20 minutes until the cookies are golden brown.

Prep Tip: This recipe makes a lot of cookies, and the amount and baking time depends on how big you like your cookies. Larger cookies tend to be a bit softer and take longer to cook, whereas smaller ones cook more quickly and are crunchier.

LEMON BUNDT
Ciambella al Limone

PREP TIME: 15 MINUTES // **COOK TIME:** 35 TO 40 MINUTES // **YIELD:** 1 CAKE / 10 TO 12 SERVINGS

Citrus fruits grow plentifully in southern Italy, and some of the tastiest lemons come from Sicily. In addition to loving their citrus, the southern people also prefer baking with olive oil as opposed to butter, making this cake one that is prepared often. The word *ciambella* refers to any cake that has a hole in it, similar to the Bundt in the United States.

> KID FRIENDLY
> FAMILY FRIENDLY
> DAIRY FREE

Nonstick cooking spray

1½ cups granulated sugar

5 large eggs

1 tablespoon lemon zest

½ cup freshly squeezed
   lemon juice

½ cup light-tasting olive oil

2 cups all-purpose flour

2 teaspoons baking powder

½ teaspoon salt

Confectioners' sugar, for dusting (optional)

1. Preheat the oven to 350°F. Spray a Bundt or angel food pan with cooking spray.

2. In a mixing bowl or the bowl of a stand mixer, combine the sugar, eggs, and zest, and whisk on medium speed for 5 minutes. Reduce the speed and add the lemon juice and oil, and mix until combined.

3. Slowly add the flour, baking powder, and salt, and mix until combined, being careful not to overmix.

4. Pour the batter into the prepared pan, and bake for 35 to 40 minutes until a toothpick comes out clean.

5. Cool completely before removing from the pan. Dust with confectioners sugar (if using).

Prep Tip: When zesting and juicing a lemon, be sure to remove the zest before juicing it.

CAPRESE CAKE
Torta Caprese

PREP TIME: 20 MINUTES // **COOK TIME:** 1 HOUR // **YIELD:** 1 CAKE / 10 SERVINGS

Believed to have been the inadvertent invention of a chef in Capri who forgot to add flour to his cake batter, this delicious gluten-free cake is favored by all who are looking for a not-so-sweet dessert to end a meal with. Chocolaty and almost fudgy, this cake is rich, so it easily serves 10 people or more. I use semisweet chocolate, but feel free to use whichever you prefer—just make sure it's excellent quality.

> KID FRIENDLY

> FAMILY FRIENDLY

> GLUTEN FREE

14 tablespoons (1¾ sticks) unsalted butter, plus more for greasing

12 ounces whole almonds

1¼ cups sugar, divided

8 ounces semisweet baking chocolate

6 large eggs, separated

1. Preheat the oven to 325°F, and butter the sides of a 9-inch springform pan. Cut a parchment paper circle to fit in the bottom of the pan.

2. In a food processor, grind the almonds and ¼ cup of sugar until finely ground.

3. Melt the chocolate and butter in the microwave in 30-second increments, stirring between increments, and paying close attention that the mixture does not burn.

4. With a mixer, beat the egg yolks for 5 minutes. With the mixer on, add the remaining 1 cup of sugar. Add the lukewarm chocolate mixture to the egg yolks and mix well. Add the ground almond mixture, stirring to incorporate.

5. In a separate bowl, beat the egg whites with a mixer until soft peaks form. Gently fold the egg whites into the cake batter.

6. Spread the cake in the prepared pan. Bake for 1 hour or until a toothpick inserted around the corners comes out clean. The cake will appear undercooked in the center. You may opt to cook it longer if you desire a more solid center.

Substitution Tip: This cake is easily adaptable; some variations include using hazelnuts or walnuts instead of the almonds, adding a few tablespoons of coffee, chocolate, or hazelnut liqueur to the batter, or adding a tablespoon of espresso powder for a mocha flavor.

ZABAGLIONE
Zabaglione

PREP TIME: 5 MINUTES // **COOK TIME:** 15 MINUTES // **YIELD:** 6 SERVINGS

While the origin of this dessert is uncertain, it is most often made with the sweet Sicilian wine, Marsala. Famous throughout Italy and all over the world, this dessert can be served by itself in small serving bowls, over some berries, in cakes as a filling, or even as a dunking vessel for biscotti. When served hot and freshly prepared, zabaglione resembles a loose cream; when refrigerated, it solidifies a bit, resembling more of a pudding. Impress your guest when you serve it; pronounce it zah-bah-YONE.

> 30 MINUTES OR LESS
> KID FRIENDLY
> FAMILY FRIENDLY
> GLUTEN FREE
> DAIRY FREE

6 large **egg yolks**
1 cup granulated sugar
¼ cup **Marsala wine**

1. In a medium glass or metal bowl, combine the egg yolks and sugar. Set the bowl over a double boiler, making sure the bowl does not touch the water in the double boiler. Over low heat, whisk the eggs and sugar constantly, making sure the mixture does not stick and the eggs don't scramble.

2. While continuously whisking, add the Marsala wine in a slow stream, whisking until the cream thickens, 10 to 15 minutes.

3. Serve in whatever way you wish: in small bowls over berries, on top of pound cake, or refrigerated and enjoyed as a pudding.

Prep Tip: *This cream can be enjoyed immediately while still hot or warm, or refrigerated for up to 8 hours. Zabaglione is best served the day it is prepared.*

CAT'S TONGUE COOKIES
Lingue di Gatto

PREP TIME: 15 MINUTES // **COOK TIME:** 7 MINUTES // **YIELD:** 24 COOKIES

Delicate and tantalizing, *Lingue di Gatto* are wafer-like biscuits typical of the region of Trentino–Alto Adige. Whereas some recipes call for just egg whites, in this region, it's customary to use the entire egg—the rest of the ingredients remain the same. For added flavor, try a dash of cinnamon, some sugar granules on top, or even some chocolate shavings. My preference is to leave the batter plain and dip half of the cookie in chocolate after baking and cooling.

> 30 MINUTES OR LESS
> KID FRIENDLY
> FAMILY FRIENDLY

½ cup all-purpose flour

¼ teaspoon salt

4 tablespoons unsalted butter, softened

½ cup sugar

1 **egg**

1 teaspoon vanilla extract

1. Preheat the oven to 350°F, and line a baking sheet with parchment paper. Set aside.

2. In a small mixing bowl, combine the flour and salt.

3. In a separate bowl with a stand mixer or with a hand mixer, combine the butter and sugar and mix until light and fluffy. Add the egg and vanilla, and beat for several minutes. Add the dry ingredients to the wet ingredients, and mix just until combined.

4. Fit a piping bag with a ½-inch tip and add the batter. You can also use a resealable bag with a ½-inch corner cut out. Pipe 3-inch long strips onto the prepared baking sheet, spacing the cookies at least 2 inches apart. Bake for 5 to 7 minutes until the edges are golden. If you wish, after the cookies are cool, dip them in melted chocolate.

Prep Tip: The butter in this recipe should be softened, so leave it on the counter for at least several hours before whipping it with the sugar.

PIZZA WITH NUTELLA AND HAZELNUTS
Pizza con Nutella e Nocciole

PREP TIME: 20 MINUTES // **COOK TIME:** 10 TO 15 MINUTES // **YIELD:** 2 MEDIUM PIZZAS OR 1 LARGE PIZZA

Created by a pastry maker in Piedmont named Pietro Ferrero and his son Michele, Nutella is a food icon in Italy. Piedmont produces some of the best hazelnuts in Italy, and this concoction was initially created as a way to extend the limited supply of cocoa with the oversupply of hazelnuts. This "pizza" is prepared at pizza shops just as often as it is at private homes, and it is very much beloved by kids of all ages.

> KID FRIENDLY
> FAMILY FRIENDLY
> VEGAN
> VEGETARIAN

1 recipe Basic Pizza Dough (page 68)

Olive oil, for greasing

1 (13-ounce) jar **Nutella hazelnut spread**

1 cup chopped **hazelnuts**

1. Prepare the pizza dough. Place the dough on one or two oiled pizza pans. Score the crusts with a fork 20 to 30 times.

2. Preheat the oven to 500°F.

3. Bake the crusts for 7 to 8 minutes until the crust has gotten some color.

4. Remove the almost-cooked crusts from the oven, and carefully and evenly spread each pizza with the Nutella. Top them with the chopped hazelnuts and bake for an additional 3 to 6 minutes until the crust is golden and the Nutella has solidified a bit.

Prep Tip: You have three options for when to add the Nutella. If added at the very beginning, you will end up with a hardened chocolate topping; following this recipe will give you a semisoft topping; adding it when you take the crusts out of the oven will give you a runny topping.

TIRAMISU
Tiramisu

PREP TIME: 20 MINUTES, PLUS 2 TO 3 HOURS TO CHILL // **COOK TIME:** NONE // **YIELD:** 8 TO 10 SERVINGS

Found in homes and restaurants both across Italy and the United States, tiramisu is a go-to dessert believed to hail from the restaurant *Le Beccherie* in Treviso, Italy, near Venice. The main ingredients change little from place to place, and the three must-haves include freshly brewed espresso, mascarpone cheese, and ladyfingers. Traditionally, this treat is prepared by creating a delicious cream using raw eggs. As some people are hesitant to consume raw eggs, this recipe replaces them with whipping cream.

> FAMILY FRIENDLY

2 to 3 cups sweetened freshly brewed espresso, plus 3 tablespoons

1 pound mascarpone cheese, at room temperature

⅓ to ½ cup confectioners' sugar

1 cup fresh heavy cream

25 to 35 ladyfinger cookies (depending on the size of your tray)

1. Pour 2 to 3 cups of espresso into a bowl. Set aside.

2. In the mixing bowl of a stand mixer or using a hand mixer, mix the mascarpone cheese, 3 tablespoons of espresso, and the confectioners' sugar until all the ingredients are well blended.

3. Add the heavy cream and mix until all the ingredients are well blended, light, and airy. Set aside.

4. Gently and quickly soak one ladyfinger cookie at a time in the reserved espresso, dipping both sides. Place the ladyfinger in a large baking dish. Continue until you have a full layer of soaked ladyfingers.

Continued

5. Spoon half of the cream over the ladyfingers, spreading evenly.

6. Dip the remaining ladyfingers in the espresso and place over the cream.

7. Spread the remaining cream evenly over the top. Refrigerate for at least 2 to 3 hours before serving.

For Your Next Visit: Headed to Italy? Why not make a stop at Le Beccherie, on Piazza Ancilotto in Treviso, and try what many say is the "original" tiramisu?

LEMON SLUSH
Lemon Granita

PREP TIME: 15 MINUTES, PLUS INACTIVE TIME // **COOK TIME:** NONE // **YIELD:** 6 TO 8 SERVINGS

Although it might appear an unlikely morning treat, lemon *granita* in Sicily is a summer-time treat enjoyed at breakfast, and also after lunch, or as an afternoon cool-off. Sicilians adore this treat in the morning along with their traditional brioche bun, and it's always made with locally grown lemons. Citrus fruits are plentiful in Sicily, and so they are used in many sweet and savory recipes. Although a bit time-consuming, as it requires some attention, this refreshing treat is worth mastering.

> KID FRIENDLY
> FAMILY FRIENDLY
> GLUTEN FREE
> DAIRY FREE

2¼ cups water

1¼ cups sugar

2¼ cups freshly squeezed lemon juice

Fresh mint leaves, for garnish

1. In a medium saucepan, bring the water to a boil. Add the sugar and stir until it fully dissolves and a clear liquid is obtained. Remove from the heat and cool completely.

2. Add the lemon juice to the sugar syrup, and mix well with a whisk. Pour the mixture into a plastic container with a lid and place it in the freezer.

3. After 30 minutes in the freezer, mix the granita with a fork, breaking any crystals that might have formed. Every 30 minutes, revisit the granita, scraping it with a fork until the desired consistency is obtained. Depending on the size of your container, this will take several hours. Serve the granitas in goblets with a fresh mint leaf.

Substitution Tip: *A preferred substitution in my household is using freshly brewed sweetened espresso instead of the lemon juice. Follow the recipe steps otherwise, and top with a fresh dollop of whipped cream right before serving.*

GLOSSARY

Alla: A dish derived from a particular region. Example: Alla Romana, Alla Pugliese, Alla Calabrese.

Antipasto: Anything served before the main meal, such as olives, cured meats, or cheeses.

Biscotti: A general term meaning "cookies," but typically refers to the twice-baked variety.

Bistecca: Any steak that is beef or veal.

Brodo: Broths, such as beef or vegetable, and red tomato-based sauces.

Cantucci: A crunchy cookie resembling biscotti, only a bit smaller.

Cartoccio: A cooking method using parchment paper.

Contorno: A side dish to meat or fish, usually vegetable based.

Cucina povera: Poor man's cooking, typically referencing non-meat-based dishes or dishes that are inexpensive to prepare.

DOP: Abbreviation for Denominazione di Origine Protetta (Protected Designation of Origin). A certification that ensures products are locally made.

Guangiale: Pork cheek frequently used in Roman dishes. Pancetta is an alternative.

La dolce vita: The sweet life. Generally referencing the ease with which Italians enjoy life.

Minestra: A general term used to reference soups or stews, generally vegetable based or with legumes.

Orecchiette: Little ears. Referencing a pasta shape resembling small earlobes.

Panino: A sandwich consisting of bread stuffed with meats, cheeses, or vegetables.

Pasta al pomodoro: A tomato-based pasta dish served all over Italy.

Pasticceria: A pastry shop or bakery serving sweets, cookies, and celebration cakes.

Pecorino: Derived from the word *pecora*, Italian for "sheep," pecorino describes cheeses made from sheep's milk.

Pizzaiola: A style of cooking using tomato sauce, oregano, and garlic.

Polenta: Ground cornmeal used as a first course or in a similar fashion to mashed potatoes.

Primo piatto: First course, usually consisting of pasta, rice, or soup.

Ragù: Meat-based tomato sauce.

Sagra: A festival celebrating a particular food. Popular all over Italy, sagre are generally celebrated in the spring or summer months.

Schiacciata: Translated literally, it means "squished" or "pressed" and is used in reference to typical Tuscan bread.

Secondo piatto: Second course served after pasta, rice, or soup, usually consisting of meat or seafood.

Trattoria: A casual-style eating establishment serving homey, simple dishes.

Umido: A cooking style with added broth or sauce.

ITALIAN COURSES

The antipasto, the primo, the secondo, the contorno, the dolce! Does every Italian meal really have five courses? Well, if you are at an Italian wedding, perhaps, but for the average family meal, it's simply not possible, conceivable, or economical to include all this food. For example, it's not unusual for a family to enjoy an antipasto and primo for lunch, and a secondo with a contorno at dinner. That said, Sundays, holidays, dinner parties, and special occasions may certainly include every course, and with some preplanning, it's far easier than you might think!

When planning a full multicourse Italian meal, some forethought will take you far. It helps to decide on a theme; for example, will it be meat, fish, or vegetarian based? Avoid combining a meat-based primo with a fish-based secondo. Also, stay away from lots of heavy courses, and if one course is on the heavier side, opt for a lighter one to balance it. Finally, selecting dishes that can be prepped during the day then cooked closer to dinnertime will make your life a lot easier and less stressful.

For example, an ideal menu for a special gathering or holiday might include:

- Cannellini cream (page 14) with some crostini or chopped vegetables makes for a light antipasto that is not going to spoil appetites before the main meal.

- A simple pasta al pomodoro (see Basic Tomato Sauce recipe, page 48) is ideal for a dinner party, as you can prep the tomato sauce beforehand, and it's light enough that it will not spoil appetites for the main course.

- Involtini di Pollo (page 112) makes a great secondo, or main course. They are beloved by all and can be rolled up beforehand.

- Roman-Style Spinach (page 25) makes a great contorno and complements the rest of the meal well, as it is light, delicious, and incredibly easy and quick to prepare.

- End the meal with some delicious Tuscan Cantucci (page 135) and Vin Santo wine to really wow your guests!

THE DIRTY DOZEN & THE CLEAN FIFTEEN™

A nonprofit environmental watchdog organization called Environmental Working Group (EWG) looks at data supplied by the US Department of Agriculture (USDA) and the Food and Drug Administration (FDA) about pesticide residues. Each year it compiles a list of the best and worst pesticide loads found in commercial crops. You can use these lists to decide which fruits and vegetables to buy organic to minimize your exposure to pesticides and which produce is considered safe enough to buy conventionally. This does not mean they are pesticide-free, though, so wash these fruits and vegetables thoroughly.

Dirty Dozen™

apples	strawberries
celery	sweet bell peppers
cherries	tomatoes
grapes	
nectarines	*Additionally, nearly*
peaches	*three-quarters of hot*
pears	*pepper samples con-*
potatoes	*tained pesticide residues*
spinach	

Clean Fifteen™

asparagus	kiwis
avocados	mangos
broccoli	onions
cabbages	papayas
cantaloupes	pineapples
cauliflower	sweet corn
eggplants	sweet peas (frozen)
honeydew melons	

MEASUREMENT CONVERSIONS

Volume Equivalents (Liquid)

US Standard	US Standard (ounces)	Metric (approximate)
2 tablespoons	1 fl. oz.	30 mL
¼ cup	2 fl. oz.	60 mL
½ cup	4 fl. oz.	120 mL
1 cup	8 fl. oz.	240 mL
1½ cups	12 fl. oz.	355 mL
2 cups or 1 pint	16 fl. oz.	475 mL
4 cups or 1 quart	32 fl. oz.	1 L
1 gallon	128 fl. oz.	4 L

Oven Temperatures

Fahrenheit	Celsius (approximate)
250°F	120°C
300°F	150°C
325°F	165°C
350°F	180°C
375°F	190°C
400°F	200°C
425°F	220°C
450°F	230°C

Volume Equivalents (Dry)

US Standard	Metric (approximate)
⅛ teaspoon	0.5 mL
¼ teaspoon	1 mL
½ teaspoon	2 mL
¾ teaspoon	4 mL
1 teaspoon	5 mL
1 tablespoon	15 mL
¼ cup	59 mL
⅓ cup	79 mL
½ cup	118 mL
⅔ cup	156 mL
¾ cup	177 mL
1 cup	235 mL
2 cups or 1 pint	475 mL
3 cups	700 mL
4 cups or 1 quart	1 L

Weight Equivalents

US Standard	Metric (approximate)
½ ounce	15 g
1 ounce	30 g
2 ounces	60 g
4 ounces	115 g
8 ounces	225 g
12 ounces	340 g
16 ounces or 1 pound	455 g

RECIPE INDEX

A

Amatriciana-Style Bucatini, 59

Angry Penne, 60

Anise Sponge, 133

B

Balsamic Vinegar Steak, 91

Basic Focaccia with Basil, 72–73

Basic Olive Bread, 80

Basic Pizza Dough, 68

Basic Tomato Sauce, 48

Basic White Risotto, 52

Basil Pesto, 50

Bean and Tuna Salad, 38

Bechamel Cream, 49

Beef in Pizza-Style Sauce, 88

Beef Ragù, 86

Beef Soup, 89

C

Cannellini Cream with Parsley, 14

Caprese Cake, 140–141

Caprese Salad, 37

Cat's Tongue Cookies, 143

Chicken Breasts with Balsamic Glaze, 110

Chicken Bundles, 112

Chicken in Red Sauce, 106

Chicken in White Wine, 111

Chicken Marsala, 108

Chicken with Peppers, 100

Chickpea Soup, 41

Clams in Broth, 124

Cod in Broth, 118

Cod with Potatoes, 122

Crispy Cauliflower, 15

D

Deviled Shrimp, 126

E

Easy Beef Braciole, 87

Eggplant Cutlets, 21

F

Focaccia with Olives and Pepper Flakes, 74–75

Focaccia with Prosciutto and Parmesan
Cheese, 78–79

Fried Mini Pizzas, 83

Fried Peppers with Potatoes, 24

G

Grape Focaccia, 76–77

Gratin-Style Swiss Chard, 27

Green Beans in Red Sauce, 22

H

Homemade Pasta, 54–55

I

Italian Easter Bread, 81–82

J

Jump-in-Your-Mouth Chicken, 103

L

Lemon Bundt, 139

Lemon Caper Chicken, 104

Lemon Slush, 148

Lentil Soup, 44

Little Ears with Broccoli Rabe and Sausage, 57

M

Margherita Pizza, 69

Marinara Pizza, 71

Mediterranean-Style Salmon, 128

Milan-Style Pork Chops, 97

Milan-Style Potatoes, 26

Molise-Style Pork with Peppers, 94

Mom's "S" Cookies, 138

Mozzarella in a Carriage, 18

Mussels in Wine and Red Sauce, 117

N

Norcina-Style Pasta, 62

O

Orange and Red Onion Salad, 36

Oven-Baked Pork Chops, 93

P

Pan Chicken with Tomato, 109

Parmesan Polenta, 28

Pasta Carbonara, 63

Pasta with Bread Crumbs, 56

Pasta with Cannellini Beans, 61

Pasta with Garlic and Olive Oil, 64

Peas with Pancetta, 23

Pizza with Nutella and Hazelnuts, 144

Pork with Olives, 92

Prosciutto-Wrapped Asparagus, 17

Q

Quick Vegetable Broth, 39

R

Reinforcement Salad, 32

Ricciarelli, 134

Rice with Peas, 53

Roasted Calabrian Chicken, 107

Roasted Sausages with Potatoes and
Bell Peppers, 95

Roman-Style Spinach, 25

S

Sausage with Mushrooms and Tomatoes, 96

Savoy Cabbage and Beans Soup, 40

Scallops with Garlic and Capers, 127

Sicilian Pesto, 51

Sicilian Salad, 35

Sicilian-Style Chicken, 105

Sicilian Swordfish, 119

Spaghetti with Clam Sauce, 58

Stuffed Mushrooms, 20

Sweet and Sour Swordfish, 121

Swordfish in Red Sauce, 120

T

Tiramisu, 145–146

Tomato, Potato, and Egg Salad, 33

Tortellini in Broth, 45

Trieste-Style Cod, 123

Trout in Foil, 125

Tuscan Bean Soup, 43

Tuscan Cantucci, 135

U

Ugly but Good, 132

V

Valdostana Cutlet, 113

Venetian Chicken, 101

W

White Pizza, 70

Wine Rings, 136–137

Z

Zabaglione, 142

Zucchini Boats, 19

INDEX

A

Almonds
  Caprese Cake, 140–141
  Ricciarelli, 134
  Tuscan Cantucci, 135
Anchovies
  Pasta with Bread Crumbs, 56
  Trieste-Style Cod, 123
  White Pizza, 70
Antipasti, 13. *See also* Appetizers
Appetizers
  Cannellini Cream with Parsley, 14
  Mozzarella in a Carriage, 18
  Prosciutto-Wrapped Asparagus, 17
  Stuffed Mushrooms, 20
  Zucchini Boats, 19
Asparagus
  Prosciutto-Wrapped Asparagus, 17

B

Balsamic vinegar, 5
Basil
  Basic Focaccia with Basil, 72–73
  Basic Tomato Sauce, 48
  Basil Pesto, 50
  Bean and Tuna Salad, 38
  Beef Ragù, 86
  Caprese Salad, 37
  frozen, 6
  Margherita Pizza, 69
  Sicilian Pesto, 51
  Sicilian Salad, 35
  Tomato, Potato, and Egg Salad, 33

Beans, 3, 5. *See also* Chickpeas
  Bean and Tuna Salad, 38
  Cannellini Cream with Parsley, 14
  Pasta with Cannellini Beans, 61
  Savoy Cabbage and Beans Soup, 40
  Tuscan Bean Soup, 43
Beef
  Balsamic Vinegar Steak, 91
  Beef in Pizza-Style Sauce, 88
  Beef Ragù, 86
  Beef Soup, 89
  Easy Beef Braciole, 87
Bell peppers
  Chicken with Peppers, 100
  Fried Peppers with Potatoes, 24
  Molise-Style Pork with Peppers, 94
  Roasted Sausages with Potatoes
    and Bell Peppers, 95
Bread crumbs, 6, 7
Breads
  Basic Focaccia with Basil, 72–73
  Basic Olive Bread, 80
  Focaccia with Olives and
    Pepper Flakes, 74–75
  Focaccia with Prosciutto and
    Parmesan Cheese, 78–79
  Grape Focaccia, 76–77
  Italian Easter Bread, 81–82
Broccoli rabe
  Little Ears with Broccoli Rabe
    and Sausage, 57
Butter, 6

C

Cabbage
  Savoy Cabbage and Beans Soup, 40

Capers, 3
  Lemon Caper Chicken, 104
  Mediterranean-Style Salmon, 128
  Reinforcement Salad, 32
  Scallops with Garlic and Capers, 127
  Sicilian Salad, 35
  Sicilian-Style Chicken, 105

Carne. *See* Beef; Pork

Carrots
  Beef Soup, 89
  Chicken Breasts with Balsamic Glaze, 110
  Chickpea Soup, 41
  Lentil Soup, 44
  Quick Vegetable Broth, 39
  Reinforcement Salad, 32
  Tortellini in Broth, 45
  Tuscan Bean Soup, 43

Cauliflower
  Crispy Cauliflower, 15
  Reinforcement Salad, 32

Celery
  Beef Soup, 89
  Lentil Soup, 44
  Quick Vegetable Broth, 39
  Tortellini in Broth, 45

Center region, xi

Cheese, 4, 7. *See also specific*

Chicken, 6
  Chicken Breasts with Balsamic Glaze, 110
  Chicken Bundles, 112
  Chicken in Red Sauce, 106
  Chicken in White Wine, 111
  Chicken Marsala, 108
  Chicken with Peppers, 100
  Jump-in-Your-Mouth Chicken, 103
  Lemon Caper Chicken, 104
  Pan Chicken with Tomato, 109
  Roasted Calabrian Chicken, 107
  Sicilian-Style Chicken, 105
  Valdostana Cutlet, 113
  Venetian Chicken, 101

Chickpeas, 3, 5
  Chickpea Soup, 41

Chocolate
  Caprese Cake, 140–141
  Ugly but Good, 132

Clams
  Clams in Broth, 124
  Spaghetti with Clam Sauce, 58

Cod
  Cod in Broth, 118
  Cod with Potatoes, 122
  Trieste-Style Cod, 123

Contorni, 13. *See also* Sides

Cooking techniques, 8–9

D

Dairy free
  Anise Sponge, 133
  Balsamic Vinegar Steak, 91
  Basic Tomato Sauce, 48
  Bean and Tuna Salad, 38
  Beef Ragù, 86
  Beef Soup, 89
  Chicken Breasts with Balsamic Glaze, 110
  Chicken in Red Sauce, 106
  Chicken in White Wine, 111
  Chicken Marsala, 108
  Chicken with Peppers, 100
  Chickpea Soup, 41
  Clams in Broth, 124
  Cod with Potatoes, 122
  Deviled Shrimp, 126

Dairy free (*Continued*)

    Fried Peppers with Potatoes, 24

    Green Beans in Red Sauce, 22

    Lemon Bundt, 139

    Lemon Caper Chicken, 104

    Lemon Slush, 148

    Lentil Soup, 44

    Mediterranean-Style Salmon, 128

    Molise-Style Pork with Peppers, 94

    Mom's "S" Cookies, 138

    Mussels in Wine and Red Sauce, 117

    Orange and Red Onion Salad, 36

    Pan Chicken with Tomato, 109

    Peas with Pancetta, 23

    Pork with Olives, 92

    Quick Vegetable Broth, 39

    Reinforcement Salad, 32

    Ricciarelli, 134

    Roasted Calabrian Chicken, 107

    Roasted Sausages with Potatoes
       and Bell Peppers, 95

    Sausage with Mushrooms and Tomatoes, 96

    Scallops with Garlic and Capers, 127

    Sicilian Salad, 35

    Sicilian-Style Chicken, 105

    Sicilian Swordfish, 119

    Sweet and Sour Swordfish, 121

    Swordfish in Red Sauce, 120

    Tomato, Potato, and Egg Salad, 33

    Trieste-Style Cod, 123

    Trout in Foil, 125

    Tuscan Cantucci, 135

    Wine Rings, 136–137

    Zabaglione, 142

Dolce. *See* Sweets

E

Eggplants

    Eggplant Cutlets, 21

Eggs

    Anise Sponge, 133

    Caprese Cake, 140–141

    Cat's Tongue Cookies, 143

    Crispy Cauliflower, 15

    Eggplant Cutlets, 21

    Homemade Pasta, 54–55

    Italian Easter Bread, 81–82

    Lemon Bundt, 139

    Milan-Style Pork Chops, 97

    Mom's "S" Cookies, 138

    Mozzarella in a Carriage, 18

    Oven-Baked Pork Chops, 93

    Pasta Carbonara, 63

    Ricciarelli, 134

    Tomato, Potato, and Egg Salad, 33

    Tuscan Cantucci, 135

    Ugly but Good, 132

    Valdostana Cutlet, 113

    Wine Rings, 136–137

    Zabaglione, 142

Equipment, 7–8

Espresso

    Tiramisu, 145–146

F

Family friendly

    Amatriciana-Style Bucatini, 59

    Anise Sponge, 133

    Balsamic Vinegar Steak, 91

    Basic Focaccia with Basil, 72–73

    Basic Olive Bread, 80

    Basic Pizza Dough, 68

    Basic Tomato Sauce, 48

    Basic White Risotto, 52

    Basil Pesto, 50

    Bechamel Cream, 49

    Beef in Pizza-Style Sauce, 88

    Beef Ragù, 86

Beef Soup, 89

Caprese Cake, 140–141

Caprese Salad, 37

Cat's Tongue Cookies, 143

Chicken Breasts with
    Balsamic Glaze, 110

Chicken Bundles, 112

Chicken in Red Sauce, 106

Chicken Marsala, 108

Chicken with Peppers, 100

Cod with Potatoes, 122

Crispy Cauliflower, 15

Easy Beef Braciole, 87

Eggplant Cutlets, 21

Focaccia with Prosciutto and
    Parmesan Cheese, 78–79

Fried Mini Pizzas, 83

Fried Peppers with Potatoes, 24

Grape Focaccia, 76–77

Homemade Pasta, 54–55

Italian Easter Bread, 81–82

Jump-in-Your-Mouth Chicken, 103

Lemon Bundt, 139

Lemon Caper Chicken, 104

Lemon Slush, 148

Little Ears with Broccoli Rabe and Sausage, 57

Margherita Pizza, 69

Marinara Pizza, 71

Mediterranean-Style Salmon, 128

Milan-Style Pork Chops, 97

Milan-Style Potatoes, 26

Molise-Style Pork with Peppers, 94

Mom's "S" Cookies, 138

Mozzarella in a Carriage, 18

Norcina-Style Pasta, 62

Oven-Baked Pork Chops, 93

Pan Chicken with Tomato, 109

Parmesan Polenta, 28

Pasta Carbonara, 63

Pasta with Bread Crumbs, 56

Pasta with Cannellini Beans, 61

Peas with Pancetta, 23

Pizza with Nutella and Hazelnuts, 144

Pork with Olives, 92

Prosciutto-Wrapped Asparagus, 17

Reinforcement Salad, 32

Ricciarelli, 134

Rice with Peas, 53

Roasted Calabrian Chicken, 107

Roasted Sausages with Potatoes
    and Bell Peppers, 95

Roman-Style Spinach, 25

Savoy Cabbage and Beans Soup, 40

Scallops with Garlic and Capers, 127

Sicilian Pesto, 51

Sicilian-Style Chicken, 105

Sicilian Swordfish, 119

Stuffed Mushrooms, 20

Tiramisu, 145–146

Tomato, Potato, and Egg Salad, 33

Tortellini in Broth, 45

Tuscan Bean Soup, 43

Tuscan Cantucci, 135

Ugly but Good, 132

Valdostana Cutlet, 113

Venetian Chicken, 101

White Pizza, 70

Wine Rings, 136–137

Zabaglione, 142

Zucchini Boats, 19

Fish

    Bean and Tuna Salad, 38

    Cod in Broth, 118

    Cod with Potatoes, 122

    Mediterranean-Style Salmon, 128

    Pasta with Bread Crumbs, 56

    Sicilian Swordfish, 119

    Sweet and Sour Swordfish, 121

Fish (*Continued*)

  Swordfish in Red Sauce, 120

  Trieste-Style Cod, 123

  Trout in Foil, 125

  White Pizza, 70

Fontina cheese

  Valdostana Cutlet, 113

Food storage, 7

Freezer staples, 6

Fruits, 2

Frutti di mare. *See* Seafood

G

Garlic, 2, 7

Gluten free

  Bean and Tuna Salad, 38

  Beef in Pizza-Style Sauce, 88

  Beef Ragù, 86

  Beef Soup, 89

  Cannellini Cream with Parsley, 14

  Caprese Cake, 140–141

  Clams in Broth, 124

  Cod in Broth, 118

  Cod with Potatoes, 122

  Deviled Shrimp, 126

  Fried Peppers with Potatoes, 24

  Green Beans in Red Sauce, 22

  Lemon Slush, 148

  Lentil Soup, 44

  Mediterranean-Style Salmon, 128

  Milan-Style Potatoes, 26

  Molise-Style Pork with Peppers, 94

  Mussels in Wine and Red Sauce, 117

  Orange and Red Onion Salad, 36

  Peas with Pancetta, 23

  Quick Vegetable Broth, 39

  Reinforcement Salad, 32

  Ricciarelli, 134

  Roasted Sausages with Potatoes and
    Bell Peppers, 95

  Sausage with Mushrooms and Tomatoes, 96

  Scallops with Garlic and Capers, 127

  Sicilian Salad, 35

  Sicilian Swordfish, 119

  Sweet and Sour Swordfish, 121

  Swordfish in Red Sauce, 120

  Tomato, Potato, and Egg Salad, 33

  Trieste-Style Cod, 123

  Ugly but Good, 132

  Zabaglione, 142

Grana Padano cheese

  Cannellini Cream with Parsley, 14

  Crispy Cauliflower, 15

  Zucchini Boats, 19

Grapes

  Grape Focaccia, 76–77

Green beans

  Green Beans in Red Sauce, 22

H

Ham. *See also* Prosciutto

  Valdostana Cutlet, 113

Hazelnuts

  Pizza with Nutella and Hazelnuts, 144

  Tuscan Cantucci, 135

  Ugly but Good, 132

I

Ingredients

  basic, 10

  canned and pickled, 3

  choosing quality, 5

  dry goods, 4

  freezer, 6

  fresh and perishable, 2

  refrigerator, 4, 6

seasonal, viii–ix

spices, 3

Insalate, 31. *See also* Salads

Islands region, xi

Italian cuisine, regional, ix–xi

K

Kid friendly

Anise Sponge, 133

Basic Focaccia with Basil, 72–73

Basic Pizza Dough, 68

Basic Tomato Sauce, 48

Basic White Risotto, 52

Basil Pesto, 50

Bechamel Cream, 49

Beef in Pizza-Style Sauce, 88

Caprese Cake, 140–141

Cat's Tongue Cookies, 143

Chicken Breasts with Balsamic Glaze, 110

Chicken Bundles, 112

Chicken with Peppers, 100

Eggplant Cutlets, 21

Focaccia with Prosciutto and
    Parmesan Cheese, 78–79

Fried Mini Pizzas, 83

Fried Peppers with Potatoes, 24

Grape Focaccia, 76–77

Homemade Pasta, 54–55

Italian Easter Bread, 81–82

Jump-in-Your-Mouth Chicken, 103

Lemon Bundt, 139

Lemon Slush, 148

Little Ears with Broccoli Rabe
    and Sausage, 57

Margherita Pizza, 69

Marinara Pizza, 71

Mom's "S" Cookies, 138

Mozzarella in a Carriage, 18

Oven-Baked Pork Chops, 93

Pan Chicken with Tomato, 109

Pasta Carbonara, 63

Pasta with Bread Crumbs, 56

Pasta with Cannellini Beans, 61

Peas with Pancetta, 23

Pizza with Nutella and Hazelnuts, 144

Prosciutto-Wrapped Asparagus, 17

Ricciarelli, 134

Rice with Peas, 53

Roasted Calabrian Chicken, 107

Tomato, Potato, and Egg Salad, 33

Tortellini in Broth, 45

Tuscan Cantucci, 135

Valdostana Cutlet, 113

Venetian Chicken, 101

White Pizza, 70

Wine Rings, 136–137

Zabaglione, 142

Zucchini Boats, 19

L

Leftovers, 7

Lemons

Bean and Tuna Salad, 38

Cannellini Cream with Parsley, 14

Lemon Bundt, 139

Lemon Caper Chicken, 104

Lemon Slush, 148

Mom's "S" Cookies, 138

Orange and Red Onion Salad, 36

Roasted Calabrian Chicken, 107

Scallops with Garlic and Capers, 127

Trout in Foil, 125

Lentils

Lentil Soup, 44

M

Mascarpone cheese
    Tiramisu, 145–146
Mint
    Lemon Slush, 148
Mozzarella cheese
    Caprese Salad, 37
    Margherita Pizza, 69
    Mozzarella in a Carriage, 18
    Zucchini Boats, 19
Mushrooms
    Chicken Marsala, 108
    Sausage with Mushrooms and Tomatoes, 96
    Stuffed Mushrooms, 20
Mussels
    Mussels in Wine and Red Sauce, 117

N

Northeast region, xi
Northwest region, xi
Nutmeg, 3
Nuts, 2. *See also* Almonds; Hazelnuts;
    Pine nuts

O

Olive oil, 3, 5
Olives
    Basic Olive Bread, 80
    Focaccia with Olives and
        Pepper Flakes, 74–75
    Mediterranean-Style Salmon, 128
    Molise-Style Pork with Peppers, 94
    Orange and Red Onion Salad, 36
    Pan Chicken with Tomato, 109
    Pork with Olives, 92
    Reinforcement Salad, 32
    Sicilian-Style Chicken, 105
    Sicilian Swordfish, 119
Onions, 2, 7

Oranges

Oranges
    Mom's "S" Cookies, 138
    Orange and Red Onion Salad, 36
    Ricciarelli, 134
    Tuscan Cantucci, 135
Oregano, 3

P

Pancetta
    Amatriciana-Style Bucatini, 59
    Milan-Style Potatoes, 26
    Pasta Carbonara, 63
    Peas with Pancetta, 23
    Rice with Peas, 53
    Savoy Cabbage and Beans Soup, 40
Pane. *See* Breads
Pantry staples, 2–4
Parmesan cheese, 4, 7
    Basic White Risotto, 52
    Basil Pesto, 50
    Cannellini Cream with Parsley, 14
    Crispy Cauliflower, 15
    Easy Beef Braciole, 87
    Eggplant Cutlets, 21
    Focaccia with Prosciutto and
        Parmesan Cheese, 78–79
    Fried Mini Pizzas, 83
    Gratin-Style Swiss Chard, 27
    Norcina-Style Pasta, 62
    Oven-Baked Pork Chops, 93
    Parmesan Polenta, 28
    Prosciutto-Wrapped Asparagus, 17
    Rice with Peas, 53
    Savoy Cabbage and Beans Soup, 40
    Sicilian Pesto, 51
    Stuffed Mushrooms, 20
    Tortellini in Broth, 45
    White Pizza, 70
    Zucchini Boats, 19

Parsley, 6

Pasta, 4, 5, 47
    Amatriciana-Style Bucatini, 59
    Angry Penne, 60
    Homemade Pasta, 54–55
    Little Ears with Broccoli Rabe
        and Sausage, 57
    Norcina-Style Pasta, 62
    Pasta Carbonara, 63
    Pasta with Bread Crumbs, 56
    Pasta with Cannellini Beans, 61
    Pasta with Garlic and Olive Oil, 64
    Spaghetti with Clam Sauce, 58
    Tortellini in Broth, 45

Peas, 6
    Peas with Pancetta, 23
    Rice with Peas, 53

Pecorino Romano cheese, 4
    Amatriciana-Style Bucatini, 59
    Angry Penne, 60
    Basil Pesto, 50
    Pasta Carbonara, 63
    Pasta with Bread Crumbs, 56
    Pasta with Garlic and Olive Oil, 64

Peperoncino, 3

Pesce. See Fish

Pine nuts
    Basil Pesto, 50
    Roman-Style Spinach, 25
    Sicilian Pesto, 51
    Sicilian Swordfish, 119

Pizza, 67
    Fried Mini Pizzas, 83
    Margherita Pizza, 69
    Marinara Pizza, 71
    Pizza with Nutella and Hazelnuts, 144
    White Pizza, 70

Pizza dough, 6
    Basic Pizza Dough, 68

Polenta, 4
    Parmesan Polenta, 28

Pollo. See Chicken

Pork. See also Ham; Pancetta; Prosciutto; Sausage
    Milan-Style Pork Chops, 97
    Molise-Style Pork with Peppers, 94
    Oven-Baked Pork Chops, 93
    Pork with Olives, 92

Potatoes, 2
    Cod in Broth, 118
    Cod with Potatoes, 122
    Fried Peppers with Potatoes, 24
    Milan-Style Potatoes, 26
    Roasted Calabrian Chicken, 107
    Roasted Sausages with Potatoes
        and Bell Peppers, 95
    Sicilian Salad, 35
    Tomato, Potato, and Egg Salad, 33
    Trieste-Style Cod, 123
    Trout in Foil, 125

Prosciutto
    Chicken Bundles, 112
    Easy Beef Braciole, 87
    Focaccia with Prosciutto and
        Parmesan Cheese, 78–79
    Jump-in-Your-Mouth Chicken, 103
    Prosciutto-Wrapped Asparagus, 17

Provolone cheese
    Chicken Bundles, 112
    Easy Beef Braciole, 87
    White Pizza, 70

R

Raisins
    Roman-Style Spinach, 25

Recipes, about, 9–10

Refrigerator staples, 4, 6

Rice, 4, 47
    Basic White Risotto, 52
    Rice with Peas, 53

Ricotta cheese
  Sicilian Pesto, 51
Rosemary
  Chicken in White Wine, 111
  Focaccia with Prosciutto and
    Parmesan Cheese, 78–79
  Fried Mini Pizzas, 83
  Lemon Caper Chicken, 104
  Pork with Olives, 92
  Roasted Calabrian Chicken, 107
  Roasted Sausages with Potatoes and
    Bell Peppers, 95

S
Sage
  Jump-in-Your-Mouth Chicken, 103
  Venetian Chicken, 101
Salads
  Bean and Tuna Salad, 38
  Caprese Salad, 37
  Orange and Red Onion Salad, 36
  Reinforcement Salad, 32
  Sicilian Salad, 35
  Tomato, Potato, and Egg Salad, 33
Salami
  Chicken Bundles, 112
  Easy Beef Braciole, 87
Salmon
  Mediterranean-Style Salmon, 128
Sauces
  Basic Tomato Sauce, 48
  Basil Pesto, 50
  Bechamel Cream, 49
  Sicilian Pesto, 51
Sausage
  Little Ears with Broccoli Rabe and Sausage, 57
  Norcina-Style Pasta, 62
  Roasted Sausages with Potatoes
    and Bell Peppers, 95

Sausage with Mushrooms and Tomatoes, 96
  Tuscan Bean Soup, 43
  Zucchini Boats, 19
Scallops
  Scallops with Garlic and Capers, 127
Seafood. *See also* Fish
  Clams in Broth, 124
  Deviled Shrimp, 126
  Mussels in Wine and Red Sauce, 117
  Scallops with Garlic and Capers, 127
  Spaghetti with Clam Sauce, 58
Seasonal cooking, viii
Shrimp
  Deviled Shrimp, 126
Sides
  Crispy Cauliflower, 15
  Eggplant Cutlets, 21
  Fried Peppers with Potatoes, 24
  Gratin-Style Swiss Chard, 27
  Green Beans in Red Sauce, 22
  Milan-Style Potatoes, 26
  Parmesan Polenta, 28
  Peas with Pancetta, 23
  Roman-Style Spinach, 25
Soups
  Beef Soup, 89
  Chickpea Soup, 41
  Lentil Soup, 44
  Quick Vegetable Broth, 39
  Savoy Cabbage and Beans Soup, 40
  Tortellini in Broth, 45
  Tuscan Bean Soup, 43
South region, xi
Spinach
  Chickpea Soup, 41
  Roman-Style Spinach, 25
Sweets
  Anise Sponge, 133
  Caprese Cake, 140–141

Cat's Tongue Cookies, 143

Lemon Bundt, 139

Lemon Slush, 148

Mom's "S" Cookies, 138

Pizza with Nutella and Hazelnuts, 144

Ricciarelli, 134

Tiramisu, 145–146

Tuscan Cantucci, 135

Ugly but Good, 132

Wine Rings, 136–137

Zabaglione, 142

Swiss chard

Gratin-Style Swiss Chard, 27

Swordfish

Sicilian Swordfish, 119

Sweet and Sour Swordfish, 121

Swordfish in Red Sauce, 120

T

30 minutes or less

Amatriciana-Style Bucatini, 59

Angry Penne, 60

Balsamic Vinegar Steak, 91

Basic Focaccia with Basil, 72–73

Basic Olive Bread, 80

Basic Pizza Dough, 68

Basic Tomato Sauce, 48

Basic White Risotto, 52

Basil Pesto, 50

Bean and Tuna Salad, 38

Bechamel Cream, 49

Beef in Pizza-Style Sauce, 88

Beef Ragù, 86

Cannellini Cream with Parsley, 14

Caprese Salad, 37

Cat's Tongue Cookies, 143

Chicken in White Wine, 111

Chicken Marsala, 108

Chickpea Soup, 41

Clams in Broth, 124

Crispy Cauliflower, 15

Deviled Shrimp, 126

Eggplant Cutlets, 21

Focaccia with Olives and Pepper Flakes, 74–75

Focaccia with Prosciutto and
    Parmesan Cheese, 78–79

Fried Mini Pizzas, 83

Fried Peppers with Potatoes, 24

Grape Focaccia, 76–77

Gratin-Style Swiss Chard, 27

Homemade Pasta, 54–55

Italian Easter Bread, 81–82

Jump-in-Your-Mouth Chicken, 103

Lemon Caper Chicken, 104

Little Ears with Broccoli Rabe and Sausage, 57

Margherita Pizza, 69

Marinara Pizza, 71

Milan-Style Pork Chops, 97

Molise-Style Pork with Peppers, 94

Mozzarella in a Carriage, 18

Mussels in Wine and Red Sauce, 117

Norcina-Style Pasta, 62

Orange and Red Onion Salad, 36

Oven-Baked Pork Chops, 93

Pan Chicken with Tomato, 109

Parmesan Polenta, 28

Pasta Carbonara, 63

Pasta with Bread Crumbs, 56

Pasta with Cannellini Beans, 61

Pasta with Garlic and Olive Oil, 64

Peas with Pancetta, 23

Pork with Olives, 92

Prosciutto-Wrapped Asparagus, 17

Reinforcement Salad, 32

Rice with Peas, 53

Roasted Sausages with Potatoes
    and Bell Peppers, 95

Roman-Style Spinach, 25

30 minutes or less *(Continued)*
    Sausage with Mushrooms and Tomatoes, 96
    Savoy Cabbage and Beans Soup, 40
    Scallops with Garlic and Capers, 127
    Sicilian Pesto, 51
    Sicilian Salad, 35
    Sicilian Swordfish, 119
    Spaghetti with Clam Sauce, 58
    Stuffed Mushrooms, 20
    Sweet and Sour Swordfish, 121
    Swordfish in Red Sauce, 120
    Tomato, Potato, and Egg Salad, 33
    Tortellini in Broth, 45
    Valdostana Cutlet, 113
    Venetian Chicken, 101
    White Pizza, 70
    Zabaglione, 142
Tomatoes
    Amatriciana-Style Bucatini, 59
    Angry Penne, 60
    Basic Tomato Sauce, 48
    Beef in Pizza-Style Sauce, 88
    Beef Ragù, 86
    Beef Soup, 89
    canned, 3, 5
    Caprese Salad, 37
    Chicken in Red Sauce, 106
    Chickpea Soup, 41
    Cod with Potatoes, 122
    Deviled Shrimp, 126
    Easy Beef Braciole, 87
    Green Beans in Red Sauce, 22
    Lentil Soup, 44
    Margherita Pizza, 69
    Marinara Pizza, 71
    Mediterranean-Style Salmon, 128
    Milan-Style Potatoes, 26
    Molise-Style Pork with Peppers, 94

Mussels in Wine and Red Sauce, 117
    Pan Chicken with Tomato, 109
    Pasta with Cannellini Beans, 61
    Quick Vegetable Broth, 39
    Sausage with Mushrooms and Tomatoes, 96
    Sicilian Pesto, 51
    Sicilian Salad, 35
    Sicilian-Style Chicken, 105
    Sicilian Swordfish, 119
    Swordfish in Red Sauce, 120
    Tomato, Potato, and Egg Salad, 33
    Tuscan Bean Soup, 43
Trout
    Trout in Foil, 125
Tuna, 5
    Bean and Tuna Salad, 38

V

Vegan
    Basic Focaccia with Basil, 72–73
    Basic Olive Bread, 80
    Basic Pizza Dough, 68
    Basic Tomato Sauce, 48
    Chickpea Soup, 41
    Focaccia with Olives and Pepper Flakes, 74–75
    Fried Peppers with Potatoes, 24
    Green Beans in Red Sauce, 22
    Lentil Soup, 44
    Marinara Pizza, 71
    Orange and Red Onion Salad, 36
    Pasta with Cannellini Beans, 61
    Pizza with Nutella and Hazelnuts, 144
    Quick Vegetable Broth, 39
    Reinforcement Salad, 32
    Sicilian Salad, 35
Vegetables. *See also specific*
    fresh, 6
    shopping for, 2

Vegetarian
  Basic Focaccia with Basil, 72–73
  Basic Olive Bread, 80
  Basic Pizza Dough, 68
  Basic Tomato Sauce, 48
  Basic White Risotto, 52
  Basil Pesto, 50
  Bechamel Cream, 49
  Cannellini Cream with Parsley, 14
  Caprese Salad, 37
  Chickpea Soup, 41
  Crispy Cauliflower, 15
  Eggplant Cutlets, 21
  Focaccia with Olives and Pepper Flakes, 74–75
  Fried Mini Pizzas, 83
  Fried Peppers with Potatoes, 24
  Grape Focaccia, 76–77
  Gratin-Style Swiss Chard, 27
  Green Beans in Red Sauce, 22
  Homemade Pasta, 54–55
  Italian Easter Bread, 81–82
  Lentil Soup, 44

  Margherita Pizza, 69
  Marinara Pizza, 71
  Mozzarella in a Carriage, 18
  Orange and Red Onion Salad, 36
  Parmesan Polenta, 28
  Pasta with Cannellini Beans, 61
  Pasta with Garlic and Olive Oil, 64
  Pizza with Nutella and Hazelnuts, 144
  Quick Vegetable Broth, 39
  Reinforcement Salad, 32
  Roman-Style Spinach, 25
  Sicilian Pesto, 51
  Sicilian Salad, 35
  Stuffed Mushrooms, 20
  Tomato, Potato, and Egg Salad, 33
Vinegars, 3, 5

Z
Zucchini
  Zucchini Boats, 19
Zuppe, 31. *See also* Soups

ACKNOWLEDGMENTS

Before I could even reach the counter, I was always welcomed in the kitchen. Far from being concerned with me burning myself, as is typical of young parents with rambunctious kids, my mother, Celeste, instead invited me into the kitchen, and I was more than happy to spend the time with her. Whether it was shelling peas, snipping green beans, or rolling some dough for her beloved "S" cookies, my fondest memories of life in Italy revolve around food and cooking. In fact, this book would have been impossible without my mom's support and culinary knowledge. Thanks, Mom, for never tiring of me asking "how much of this?" and "how do you do that?" questions!

To my sister, Roseanne, the real writer in the family: Thank you for always insisting I write a cookbook. Your dedication to writing has compelled me to put pen to paper and really, finally do it. Thank you for passing on some of your recipes and showing me your tricks and tips. This book wouldn't have been possible without you and Mom supporting and believing in me—far more than I believed in myself.

To my dad, Giovanni, who should have been a chef but never got the chance, thank you for instilling in me an appreciation for both cooking and eating.

To my many clients, both from my cooking classes and culinary tours—thank you for allowing me to come into your lives and show you my food, culture, history, and my Italy. Thank you for listening to my stories about my upbringing in Calabria and for entrusting me enough to spend a full week with me in Italy. I look forward to many more classes and trips together!

ABOUT THE AUTHOR

Francesca Montillo was born in Italy and currently lives and travels between Boston and her native country.

In 2016, Francesca combined her two passions, Italian food and Italian travel, and started *Lazy Italian Culinary Adventures* (TheLazyItalian.com). As a culinary instructor and culinary tour leader in Italy, she teaches her students recipes that are uncomplicated, straightforward, and easy to make at home.

It is during her trips back to Italy that Francesca feels her soul soaring. Through her culinary adventures, Francesca is able to showcase the cuisine of her native country by bringing students and travelers to the source. On her tours, travelers partake in cooking classes with locals, visit honey and cheese farms, learn the olive oil–making process, and enjoy picnics at stunning vineyards. Francesca expertly designs all adventures, and some of her favorite destinations include the cities of Bologna, Verona, and Florence, and the southern regions of Puglia, Sicily, and Calabria.

Francesca is also a freelance food and travel writer whose work has appeared on Huffington Post, Tastes of Italia, Foodies of New England, Italian Sons and Daughters of America, and several other notable outlets. *Lazy Italian Culinary Adventures* has been featured in the *Boston Globe*, *Success Magazine*, *Wicked Local*, *Boston Voyager*, and *Medium*, to name a few, as well as local TV shows. For information on cooking classes or culinary adventures to Italy, visit Francesca at TheLazyItalian.com.

CPSIA information can be obtained
at www.ICGtesting.com
Printed in the USA
BVHW090603020119
536792BV00022B/261/P